C000091036

# The **Dua book** for living in accordance with Islam

Authentic prayers of supplication and thanksgiving for all situations in life

Duas for success, health, protection and spiritual growth
(islamic books)

**Ibrahim Al-Abadi & Islam Way**

**ORIGINAL FIRST EDITION**

ISBN: 978-3-98929-999-3

**IMPRINT:**
BOOK SHELTER GMBH
AUFHÄUSERSTRASSE 64
30457 HANOVER
GERMANY

# TABLE OF CONTENTS

## Prayers for protection     30

## Prayers for support     43

# Foreword

الحمد الله

We are pleased that you have chosen to read this book and draw closer to Allah.

We are awaited by over 250 Du'ā', various praises and creeds that have been handed down to us in the sacred texts of Islam.

Du'ā' has several meanings: Worship, supplication, call for help and wish. In general, a Du'ā' is a wish that we make to Allah in order to come closer to Him and glorify Him.

The Prophet Muhammad ﷺ said:

"The two words that are the easiest to pronounce on the tongue, the heaviest on the scales, and the most beloved to the Most Merciful are, "Praise be to Allah, praise be to Him, praise be to Allah, the Exalted.""

Source: Al-Bukhari 7/168 and Muslim 4/2072.

We also use Du'ā' to ask the Almighty for help and support in everyday life and in difficult situations. For example, to overcome weaknesses of character.

"O Allah, I seek refuge in You from evil traits, deeds and instincts".

Source: Jami' at-Tirmidhi 3591

It is important not to confuse Du'ā' with the actual Muslim obligatory prayer. In contrast to Du'ā', which we can use at any time of the day and invoke Allah's assistance, the prayer is performed at fixed times five times a day. Du'ā' can therefore be used flexibly and we can ask for Allah's support or praise Him whenever we deem it appropriate. The aim of Du'ā' here is not to constantly count on Allah's help, but to be close to him and thus live and master the often difficult everyday life more calmly.

Before reciting a du'ā' and in order for it to be accepted by Allah, it is advisable to first perform his ablutions (wudu). Of course, this is not possible under all circumstances and in all situations. Before reciting a Du'ā', we should raise our hands and begin by praising Allah and wishing blessings on the Prophet Muhammad ﷺ. Our palms should be facing the face. We must be careful not to ask for sinful requests or wishes or other inappropriate things. It is equally important to say the words in clear and understandable language. That is why we find the corresponding audio file for each Du'ā' in this book, which we can easily access with our smartphone. All we need is an internet connection. For each Du'ā' we will also find the original Arabic text, the German translation and a precise phonetic transcription, which, together with the audio files, will help us to perfect our Arabic pronunciation.

After reciting a Du'ā', one must be patient. Allah does not always respond directly to a supplication. The Almighty does so at the time that seems most appropriate to Him. Of course, it may happen that the result or Allah's answer to a Du'ā' is received immediately and directly. However, it is also possible that the result will only occur at an as yet unknown time in the future or even in the next life - i.e. after the time that seems best to Allah.

We hope you enjoy studying and reciting the Du'ā' in this book. May the Almighty fulfill your praises, wishes and prayers.

Let us start, with the blessing of Allah.

لنبدأ على بركة الله.

# Prayers for specific everyday situations

## 01 PRAYER UPON PUTTING ON CLOTHES

اللَّهمَّ لَكَ الحمدُ أنتَ كسوتَنيهِ، أسألُكَ خيرَه، وخيرَ ما صُنعَ لَه، وأعوذُ بِكَ من شرِّه، وشرِّ ما صُنِعَ لَهُ.

Arabic

Allāhumma lakal-ḥamdu 'anta kasawtanīhi, 'as'aluka min khayrihi wa khayri mā ṣuni`a lahu, wa 'a`oothu bika min sharrihi wa sharri mā ṣuni`a lahu.

Phonetic transcription

O Allah, all praise is due to You. You have clothed me in it. I ask You for its goodness and the goodness of what it's made for. I seek refuge in You from its evil and the evil of what it's made for.

English

Reference: Abu Dawud and At-Tirmidhi. See also Al-Albani, Mukhtasar Shama'il At-Tirmidhi, p. 47

## 02 PRAYER WHILE LEAVING THE HOUSE

بِسْمِ اللهِ تَوَكَّلْتُ عَلَى اللهِ وَلا حَوْلَ وَلا قُوَّةَ إلاَّ بِاللهِ.

Arabic

Bismillāhi, tawakkaltu `alallāhi, wa lā ḥawla wa lā quwwata illā billāh.

Phonetic transcription

In the name of Allah, I place my trust in Allah. There is no power and no strength except with Allah.

English

Reference: Abu Dawud 4/325, At-Tirmidhi 5/490. See also Al-Albani, Sahih At-Tirmidhi 3/151

## 03 PRAYER BEFORE EATING

بِسْمِ اللهِ.

Arabic

Bismillāhi.

Phonetic transcription

In the Name of Allah.

English

Reference: Abu Dawud 4/325

## 04 PRAYER WHEN YOU LEAVE A CITY

رَبَّنَآ أَخْرِجْنَا مِنْ هَٰذِهِ ٱلْقَرْيَةِ ٱلظَّالِمِ أَهْلُهَا وَٱجْعَل لَّنَا مِن لَّدُنكَ وَلِيًّا وَٱجْعَل لَّنَا مِن لَّدُنكَ نَصِيرًا.

Arabic

Rabbana akhrijna min hadhihi lqaryati zzalimi ahluha wajal lana min ladunka waliyyan wajal lana min ladunka naṣira.

Our Lord, take us out from this town whose people are oppressors, and appoint for us from Yourself a protector and appoint for us from Yourself a helper.

Phonetic transcription

Reference: Surat An-Nisa (4:75)

English

## 05 PRAYER BEFORE WEARING NEW CLOTHES

الْبَسْ جَدِيدًا وَ عِشْ حَمِيدًا وَمُتْ شَهِيدًا.

Arabic

Ilbas jadīdan, wa `ish ḥamīdan, wa mut shahīdan.

Put on new clothes, live a praise-worthy life and die as a martyr.

Phonetic transcription

Reference: Ibn Majah 2/1178, Al-Baghawi 12/41. See also Al-Albani, Sahih Ibn Majah 2/275

English

## 06 PRAYER FOR ALLAH'S GOODWILL WHEN ENTERING A HOUSE

اللَّهُمَّ إِنِّي أَسْأَلُكَ خَيْرَ الْمَوْلَجِ، وَخَيْرَ الْمَخْرَجِ، بِسْمِ اللهِ وَلَجْنَا، وَبِسْمِ اللهِ خَرَجْنَا، وَ عَلَى اللهِ رَبِّنَا تَوَكَّلْنَا.

Arabic

Allahumma inni as'aluka khayral mawlaji wa khayral makhraj- Bismil-lahi walajna, wabismil-lahi kharajna, waAAala rabbina tawakkalna.

O Allah, I ask You for the best entrance and the best exit. In the name of Allah, we enter, and in the name of Allah, we exit, and upon Allah, our Lord, we rely.

Phonetic transcription

Reference: Abu Dawud transmitted it. Mishkat al-Masabih 2444

English

## 07 PRAYER FOR ALLAH'S HELP BEFORE EMBARKING ON A JOURNEY

اللَّهُمَّ صَاحِبْنَا فَأَفْضِلْ عَلَيْنَا، عَائِذًا بِاللَّهِ مِنَ النَّارِ.

Arabic

Alla:humma sa:ħibna: fafdil ʕalaɪna:, ʕaa:idan bɪlla:hi mina nna:r.

O Allah, accompany us and be gracious to us, I seek refuge in Allah from Hell.

Phonetic transcription

Reference: Muslim 4/2086

English

## 08 PRAYER FOR ALLAH'S SUPPORT WHEN TRAVELLING IN A SHIP

بِسْمِ اللَّهِ مَجْرَاهَا وَمُرْسَاهَا ۚ إِنَّ رَبِّي لَغَفُورٌ رَّحِيمٌ.

Arabic

bismi Allahi majraha wamursaha inna rabbee laghafoorun raheemun.

In the name of Allah, its course and its anchor. Indeed, my Lord is Forgiving, Merciful.

Phonetic transcription

Reference: Surat Hud (11:41)

English

## 09 PRAYER DURING RAIN

اللَّهُمَّ صَيِّبًا نَافِعًا.

Arabic

Allāhumma ṣayyiban nāfi`a.

Oh Allah, grant us a beneficial rain.

Phonetic transcription

Reference: Al-Bukhari, cf. Al-Asqalani, Fathul-Bari 2/518

English

## 10 PRAYER UPON DRINKING WATER

الْحَمْدُ لِلهِ الَّذِي لَمْ يَجْعَلْهُ أُجَاجاً بِذُنُوبِنَا وَ جَعَلَهُ عَذْباً فُرَاتاً بِنِعْمَتِهِ.

Arabic

Alhamdu lillaa hillazi lam yaj' alhu milhan ujaajan bi-dhunoobina wa j' alhu eadhbaan furataan biniematihi.

Reference: (Tabrani)

Praise be to Allah, who did not make it salty due to our sins, but made it fresh and plentiful by His grace.

Phonetic transcription

English

## 11 PRAYERS FOR WELL-BEING UPON ARRIVAL AT A PLACE

اللهُمَّ رَبَّ السَّمَوَاتِ السَّبْعِ وَمَا أَظْلَلْنَ، وَرَبَّ الْأَرْضِينَ السَّبْعِ وَمَا أَقْلَلْنَ، وَرَبَّ الشَّيَاطِينِ وَمَا أَضْلَلْنَ، وَرَبَّ الرِّيَاحِ وَمَا ذَرَيْنَ، فَإِنَّا نَسْأَلُكَ خَيْرَ هَذِهِ الْقَرْيَةِ وَخَيْرَ أَهْلِهَا، وَنَعُوذُ بِكَ مِنْ شَرِّهَا وَشَرِّ أَهْلِهَا وَشَرِّ مَا فِيهَا.

Arabic

Allāhumma Rabbas-samāwātis-sab`i wa mā aẓlaln, Wa Rabba 'l-arāḍīnas-sab`i wa mā aqlaln, wa Rabbash-shayāṭīni wa mā aḍlaln, wa Rabbar-riyāḥi wa mā dharayn. As'aluka khayra hādhihi 'l-qaryah, wa khayra ahlihā, wa khayra māfīhā, wa a`ūdhu bika min sharrihā, wa sharri ahlihā, wa sharri mā fīhā.

Reference: Ibn As-Sunni (no. 524)

O Allah, Lord of the seven heavens and all they overshadow, Lord of the seven worlds and all they uphold, Lord of the devils and all they lead astray, Lord of the winds and all they scatter. I ask You for the goodness of this town, and for the goodness of its people, and for the goodness it contains. I seek refuge in You from its evil, from the evil of its people, and from the evil it contains.

Phonetic transcription

English

## 12 PRAYER UPON SEEING A FIRE

إِذَا رَأَيْتُمُ الْحَرِيقَ فَكَبِّرُوا فَإِنَّ التَّكْبِيرَ يُطْفِئُهُ.

Arabic

Ida ra aitumu lħariq fa kabbiru fa ınna takbira yutfi oho.

Reference: al-Tabarani in al-Du'a (1/307)

When You see a fire, say 'Allahu Akbar,' for indeed, the act of saying 'Allahu Akbar' extinguishes it.

Phonetic transcription

English

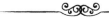

## 13 PRAYER WHEN GETTING MARRIED OR BUYING AN ANIMAL

اللَّهُمَّ إِنِّي أَسْأَلُكَ خَيْرَهَا وَخَيْرَ مَا جَبَلْتَهَا عَلَيْهِ وَأَعُوذُ بِكَ مِنْ شَرِّهَا وَمِنْ شَرِّ مَا جَبَلْتَهَا عَلَيْهِ.

Arabic

Allāhumma innī as'aluka khayrahā wa khayra mā jabaltahā `alayh, wa a`ūdhu bika min sharrihā wa sharri mā jabaltahā `alayh.

O Allah, I ask You for its goodness, and the goodness upon which You have created it, and I seek refuge in You from its evil, and from the evil upon which You have created it.

Reference: Abu Dawud 2/248 and Ibn Majah 1/617

Phonetic transcription

English

## 14 PRAYER FOR THE RETURN OF A LOST ITEM

اللهُمَّ رَادَّ الضَّالَّةِ، وَهَادِيَ الضَّلَالَةِ تَهْدِي مِنَ الضَّلَالَةِ، ارْدُدْ عَلَيَّ ضَالَّتِي بِقُدْرَتِكِ وَسُلْطَانِكَ، فَإِنَّهَا مِنْ عَطَائِكَ وَفَضْلِكَ.

Arabic

Allahumma radda dallati, wa hadiya dalalati tahdi mina dalalati, urdud 'alayya dallati bi qudratika wa sultanika fa innaha min 'ata-ika wa fadlika.

O Allah, the Turner of hearts, guide me among those who have gone astray. Direct my lost soul through Your power and authority, for it is by Your grace and favor.

Phonetic transcription

Reference: ad-Da'awat al-Kabir 556 (al-Bayhaqi)

English

## 15 PRAYER WHEN DRINKING MILK

اللَّهُمَّ بَارِكْ لَنَا فِيهِ وَزِدْنَا مِنْهُ.

Arabic

Allāhumma bārik lanā fīhi, wa zidnā minh.

O Allah, bless it for us and increase it for us.

Phonetic transcription

Reference: At-Tirmidhi 5/506. See also Al-Albani, Sahih At-Tirmidhi 3/158

English

## 16 PRAYER FOR PAYING OFF A DEBT

اللَّهُمَّ اكْفِنِي بِحَلَالِكَ عَنْ حَرَامِكَ وَأَغْنِنِي بِفَضْلِكَ عَمَّنْ سِوَاكَ.

Arabic

Allāhumma k-finī biḥalālika `an ḥarāmik, wa 'aghninī bi faḍlika `amman siwāk.

Phonetic transcription

Reference: At-Tirmidhi 5/560. See also Al-Albani, Sahih At-Tirmidhi 3/180

O Allah, suffice me with what is lawful from what is forbidden, and enrich me with Your grace beyond anyone else.

English

## 17 PRAYER FOR BLESSING A PERSON WHO GREETS

وَفِيكَ بَارَكَ اللَّهُ.

Arabic

Wafīka bārakallāhu.

Phonetic transcription

Reference: Ibn As-Sunni, p. 138, (no. 278)

And may Allah bless You.

English

## 18 PRAYER BEFORE MARITAL INTERCOURSE

بِسْمِ اللهِ اللَّهُمَّ جَنِّبْنَا الشَّيْطَانَ وَجَنِّبْ الشَّيْطَانَ مَا رَزَقْتَنَا.

Arabic

Bismillāh. Allāhumma jannibna Shayṭāna, wa jannibi Shayṭāna mā razaqtanā.

Phonetic transcription

Reference: Al-Bukhari 6/141, Muslim 2/1028

In the name of Allah. O Allah, protect us from Satan and keep Satan away from what You have provided for us.

English

## 19 PRAYER UPON HAVING MISFORTUNE

إِنَّا لِلَّهِ وَإِنَّا إِلَيْهِ رَاجِعُونَ عِنْدَ اللهِ احْتَسَبْتُ مُصِيبَتِي فَأْجُرْنِي فِيهَا.

Arabic

Innā lillāhi wa innā ilaihi rāji`ūn, Allāhumma `indaka aḥtasibu muṣībatī fa'jurnī fīhā.

Indeed, to Allah we belong, and to Him we shall return. I have placed my trust in Allah in the face of my affliction, so reward me for it.

Phonetic transcription

Reference: Jami` at-Tirmidhi 3511

English

## 20 PRAYER WHEN ENTERING THE TOILET

بِسْمِ اللَّهِ، اللَّهُمَّ إِنِّي أَعُوذُ بِكَ مِنَ الْخُبثِ وَالْخَبَائِثِ.

Arabic

Bismillāhi Allāhumma 'innī 'a`ūdhu bika minal-khubthi walkhabā'ith.

In the name of Allah, O Allah, I seek refuge in You from all that is impure and wicked.

Phonetic transcription

Reference: Al-Bukhari 1/45, Muslim 1/283

English

## 21 PRAYER FOR A BLESSED PLACE ON A TRIP

رَّبِّ أَنزِلْنِي مُنزَلًا مُّبَارَكًا وَأَنتَ خَيْرُ الْمُنزِلِينَ.

Arabic

Rabbi anzilnee munzalam mubaarakanw wa Anta khairu lmunzileen.

O my Lord, place me in a blessed abode, for You are the best of those who provide a place to stay.

Phonetic transcription

Reference: Surat Al-Mu'minunVerse 29

English

## 22 PRAYER BY THE END OF A MEETING

سُبْحَانَكَ اللهُمَّ وَبِحَمْدِكَ، أَشْهَدُ أن لا إلَهَ إِلَّا أَنْتَ أَسْتَغْفِرُكَ وَأَتُوبُ إِليك.

Arabic

Subḥānaka Allāhumma wa biḥamdika, 'ash-hadu 'an lā 'ilāha 'illā 'Anta, 'astaghfiruka wa 'atūbu 'ilayk.

Glory be to You, O Allah, and with Your praise. I bear witness that there is no god but You. I seek Your forgiveness and turn to You in repentance.

Phonetic transcription

Reference: An-Nasa'i, 'Amalul-Yawm wal-Laylah, p. 173

English

## 23 PRAYER WHILE ASCENDING/DESCENDING DURING A TRIP

عن جابر رضي الله عنه قَالَ: كُنَّا إِذَا صَعِدْنَا كَبَّرْنَا، وَإِذَا نَزَلْنَا سَبَّحْنَا.

Arabic

qāla jābiru raḍiya-llāhu ʕanhu: kunnā idhā ṣaʕadnā kabarnā, wa-idhā nazalnā sabbaḥnā.

Jabir (may Allah be pleased with him) said: "When we ascended, we would say 'Allahu Akbar' (Allah is the Greatest), and when we descended, we would say 'Subhanallah' (Glory be to Allah)."

Phonetic transcription

Reference: Al-Bukhari, cf. Al-Asqalani, Fathul-Bari 6/135

English

## 24 PRAYER WHEN GREETING

السَّلَامُ عَلَيْكُمْ وَرَحْمَةُ اللهِ وَبَرَكَاتُهُ.

Arabic

Assalāmu `alaykum wa raḥmatu llāhi wa barakātuh.

May peace, blessings, and mercy of Allah be upon You.

Phonetic transcription

Reference: al-Adab al-Mufrad 987 (al-Buchari), Sunan Abi Dawud 997

English

## 25 PRAYER BEFORE EATING A MEAL

¡اللَّهُمَّ بَارِكْ لَنَا فِيهِ وَأَطْعِمْنَا خَيْرًا مِنْهُ!

Arabic

Allāhumma bārik lanā fīhi, wa aṭ`imnā khayran minhu.

O Allah, bless it for us and provide us with something better.

Phonetic transcription

Reference:
At-Tirmidhi 5/506

English

## 26 PRAYER BEFORE DRINKING

¡اللَّهُمَّ بَارِكْ لَنَا فِيهِ وَزِدْنَا مِنْهُ!

Arabic

Allāhumma bārik lanā fīhi, wa zidnā minhu.

O Allah, bless it for us and give us more of it.

Phonetic transcription

Reference: At-Tirmidhi 5/506.
See also Al-Albani, Sahih
At-Tirmidhi 3/158

English

## 27 PRAYER FOR THE PROTECTION OF A PERSON WHO IS TRAVELLING

أَسْتَوْدِعُ اللَّهَ دِينَكَ وَأَمَانَتَكَ وَخَوَاتِيمَ عَمَلِكَ.

Arabic

Astawdi`u llāha dīnaka, wa amānataka, wa khawātīma `amalika.

I entrust to Allah Your religion, Your faith, and the outcomes of Your deeds.

Phonetic transcription

Reference: Ahmad 2/7,
At-Tirmidhi 5/499

English

# Prayers for forgiveness

## 28 PRAYER FOR FORGIVENESS AFTER COMMITTING A SIN

اللهُمَّ اغْفِرْ لِي مَا قَدَّمْتُ وَمَا أَخَّرْتُ، وَمَا أَسْرَرْتُ وَمَا أَعْلَنْتُ، وَمَا أَنْتَ أَعْلَمُ بِهِ مِنِّي، أَنْتَ الْمُقَدِّمُ وَأَنْتَ الْمُؤَخِّرُ، وَأَنْتَ عَلَى كُلِّ شَيْءٍ قَدِيرٌ.

Arabic

Allahumma, ighfir li ma qaddamtu wa ma akhkhartu, wa ma asrartu wa ma a'alantu, wa ma anta a'lamu bihi minni. Anta al-muqaddim wa anta al-mu'akhkhir, wa anta 'ala kulli shay'in qadeer.

Phonetic transcription

Reference: Muslim 1/534

O Allah, forgive me for what I have done in the past and what I will do in the future, what I have concealed and what I have made public, and what You know better about me than I do. You are the One who brings forward and delays, and You are capable of everything.

English

## 29 PRAYER FOR FORGIVENESS JUST BEFORE DEATH

اللَّهُمَّ اغْفِرْ لِي وَارْحَمْنِي وَأَلْحِقْنِي بِالرَّفِيقِ الاعلى.

Arabic

Allāhumma'ghfir lī warḥamnī wa alḥiqnī bir-rafīqi 'l-'A`alā.

Phonetic transcription

Reference: Al-Bukhari 7/10, Muslim 4/1893

O Allah, forgive me and have mercy upon me, and join me with the highest companions (in Paradise).

English

## 30 PRAYER FOR FORGIVENESS AND SUPPORT

رَبَّنَا ٱغْفِرْ لَنَا ذُنُوبَنَا وَإِسْرَافَنَا فِيٓ أَمْرِنَا وَثَبِّتْ أَقْدَامَنَا وَٱنصُرْنَا عَلَى ٱلْقَوْمِ ٱلْكَٰفِرِينَ.

Arabic

Rabbana ighfir lana thunoobana waisrafana fee amrina wathabbit aqdamana wansurna ala alqawmi alkafireena.

Phonetic transcription

Reference: Surat Al-Imran (3:147)

O Allah, forgive us our sins and our extravagance in our affairs, plant firmly our feet, and grant us victory over disbelieving people.

English

## 31 PRAYER FOR MERCY IN DIFFICULT SITUATIONS

اللَّهُمَّ رَحْمَتَكَ أَرْجُو فَلاَ تَكِلْنِي إِلَى نَفْسِي طَرْفَةَ عَيْنٍ وَأَصْلِحْ لِي شَأْنِي كُلَّهُ لاَ إِلَهَ إِلاَّ أَنْتَ.

Arabic

Allāhumma raḥmataka arjū falā takilnī ilā nafsī ṭarfata ʿayn, wa aṣliḥ lī sha'nī kullahu, lā ilāha illā anta.

Phonetic transcription

Reference: Abu Dawud 4/324, Ahmad 5/42

O Allah, I hope for Your mercy, so do not leave me to myself even for the blink of an eye. Rectify all of my affairs for me; there is no deity except You.

English

## 32 PRAYER FOR FORGIVENESS OF MISDEEDS AND SINS

رَّبَّنَآ إِنَّنَا سَمِعْنَا مُنَادِيًا يُنَادِي لِلْإِيمَٰنِ أَنْ ءَامِنُواْ بِرَبِّكُمْ فَـَٔامَنَّاۚ رَبَّنَا فَٱغْفِرْ لَنَا ذُنُوبَنَا وَكَفِّرْ عَنَّا سَيِّـَٔاتِنَا
وَتَوَفَّنَا مَعَ ٱلْأَبْرَارِ ، رَبَّنَا وَءَاتِنَا مَا وَعَدتَّنَا عَلَىٰ رُسُلِكَ وَلَا تُخْزِنَا يَوْمَ ٱلْقِيَٰمَةِۗ إِنَّكَ لَا تُخْلِفُ ٱلْمِيعَادَا.

Arabic

Rabbana innana sami'na munadiyan yunadi lil-eeman, an aminu birabbikum fa-amanna. Rabbana faghfir lana dhunubana wa kaffir 'anna sayyi'atina wa tawaffana ma'al-abrar. Rabbana wa atina ma wa'adtana 'ala rusulika wa la tukhzina yawmal-qiyamah. Innaka la tukhliful mi'aad.

Phonetic transcription

Reference: Surat Al-Imran (3:193)

Our Lord, indeed we have heard a caller calling to faith, [saying], 'Believe in Your Lord,' and we have believed. O Allah, so forgive us our sins, remove from us our misdeeds and cause us to die with the righteous. O Allah, grant us what You promised us through Your messengers and do not disgrace us on the Day of Resurrection. Indeed, You never fail in Your promise.

English

## 33 PRAYER FOR FORGIVENESS OF THE VARIOUS COMMITTED WRONGDOINGS

رَبِّ اغْفِرْ لي خَطِيئَتي وجَهْلِي، وإسْرَافِي في أمْرِي كُلِّهِ، وما أنْتَ أعْلَمُ به مِنِّي، اللَّهُمَّ اغْفِرْ لي
خَطَايَايَ، وعَمْدِي وجَهْلِي وهَزْلِي، وكُلُّ ذلكَ عِندِي .

Arabic

Rabbi-ghfir-li khati 'ati wa jahli wa israfi fi `amri kullihi, wa ma anta a'lamu bihi minni. Allahumma ighfir li khatayaya wa 'amdi, wa jahli wa jiddi wa hazli, wa kullu dhalika'indi.

Phonetic transcription

Reference: Sahih al-Bukhari 6398

My Lord, forgive me for my mistakes and ignorance, and for my excesses in all my affairs, and what You know better about me than I do. O Allah, forgive me for my sins, both deliberate and unintentional, for my ignorance, jesting, and all of that that I do.

English

## 34 PRAYER FOR REPENTANCE (TAUBAH)

أَسْتَغْفِرُ اللَّهَ وَأَتُوبُ إِلَيْهِ.

Arabic

Astaghfiru llāha wa atūbu ilayh.

Phonetic transcription

Reference: Al-Bukhari, cf. Al-Asqalani, Fathul-Bari 11/101, Muslim 4/2075

I seek the forgiveness of Allah and repent to Him.

English

## 35 PRAYER FOR FORGIVENESS & DECLARATION OF SINCERITY

سَمِعْنَا وَأَطَعْنَا ۖ غُفْرَانَكَ رَبَّنَا وَإِلَيْكَ ٱلْمَصِيرُ.

Arabic

Sami'na wa ata'na, ghufraanaka Rabbana, wa ilayka al-maseer.

Phonetic transcription

Reference: Surat Al-Baqarah (2:285)

We have heard and we obey; we seek Your forgiveness, our Lord. To You is the final return.

English

## 36 PRAYER FOR FORGIVENESS AFTER A MISSTEP

رَّبَّنَا عَلَيْكَ تَوَكَّلْنَا وَإِلَيْكَ أَنَبْنَا وَإِلَيْكَ ٱلْمَصِيرُ، رَبَّنَا لَا تَجْعَلْنَا فِتْنَةً لِّلَّذِينَ كَفَرُوا۟ وَٱغْفِرْ لَنَا رَبَّنَآ ۖ إِنَّكَ أَنتَ ٱلْعَزِيزُ ٱلْحَكِيمُ.

Arabic

Rabbana 'alaika tawakkalna wa ilayka anabna wa ilayka al-maseer. Rabbana la taj'alna fitnatan lilladhina kafaru wa ghfir lana Rabbana. Innaka anta al-Azizul-Hakeem.

Phonetic transcription

Reference: Surat Al-Mumtahanah (60:4-5)

O Allah, upon You we have relied, and to You we have turned, and to You is the destination. O Allah, do not make us objects of torment for the disbelievers and forgive us. O Allah indeed, You are the Allmight and the Wisest.

English

# 37 PRAYER FOR FORGIVENESS & REPENT

سُبْحَانَكَ وبِحَمْدِكَ، أَسْتَغْفِرُكَ وأَتُوبُ إِلَيْكَ.

Arabic

Subḥānaka Allāhumma wa biḥamdika, 'ash-hadu 'an lā 'ilāha 'illā 'Anta, 'astaghfiruka wa 'atūbu 'ilayk.

Phonetic transcription

Reference: An-Nasa'i, 'Amalul-Yawm wal-Laylah, p. 173

Glory is to You, O Allah, and praise; I bear witness that there is none worthy of worship but You. I seek Your forgiveness and turn to You in repentance.

English

# 38 PRAYER FOR FORGIVENESS AND RETRACTION OF PUNISHMENT

إِنَّمـا أنا بشرٌ فَلا تُعاقِبني، أيما رجلٌ مِن المؤمنين آذيتُه أو شتَمتُه فَلا تُعاقِبني فِيه.

Arabic

Inama 'ana bashar fala tuaqibni, 'ayuma rajulun min almuminin adhaytuh 'aw shatamtuh fala tuaqibni fihi.

Phonetic transcription

Reference: Al-Adab Al-Mufrad 613

O Allah, I am only human, so do not punish me. If I have harmed or insulted any believer, do not punish me for that.

English

# 39 PRAYER FOR FORGIVENESS OF DISBELIEF

رَبِّ إِنِّي ظَلَمْتُ نَفْسِي وَأَسْلَمْتُ مَعَ سُلَيْمَٰنَ لِلَّهِ رَبِّ ٱلْعَٰلَمِينَ.

Arabic

Rabbi innee dalamtu nafsee wa aslamtu ma'a Sulaimaana lillaahi Rabbi l 'aalameena.

Phonetic transcription

Reference: Surat An-Naml (27:44)

My Lord, indeed I have wronged myself, and I have submitted with Solomon to Allah, the Lord of all worlds.

English

## 40 PRAYER FOR FORGIVENESS FOR ALL SINS

اللَّهُمَّ اغفِر لي ذنبي كُلَّهُ دِقَّهُ، وجِلَّهُ، وأوَّلَهُ وآخِرَهُ وعلانيتَهُ وسِرَّهُ.

Arabic

Allāhumma'ghfir lī dhanbī kullahu, diqqahu wa jillahu, wa awwalahu wa ākhirahu wa sirrahu wa `alāniyyatahu.

O Allah, forgive me all my sins, great and small, the first and the last, those that are apparent and those that are hidden.

Phonetic transcription

Reference: Muslim 1/350

English

## 41 PRAYER FOR FORGIVENESS (1)

رَبِّ اغْفِرْ لِي رَبِّ اغْفِرْ لِي.

Arabic

Rabbi 'ghfir lī, Rabbi 'ghfir lī.

O Allah, forgive me. O Allah, forgive me.

Phonetic transcription

Reference: Abu Dawud 1/231

English

## 42 PRAYER FOR FORGIVENESS (2)

رَبِّ اغْفِرْ لِي وَتُبْ عَلَيَّ إِنَّكَ أَنْتَ التَّوَّابُ الْغَفُورُ.

Arabic

Rabbigh 'fir lī wa tub `alay innaka anta Tawwābu 'l-Ghafūr.

O Allah, forgive me, and accept my repentance, You are the Most-Relenting, Most-Merciful.

Phonetic transcription

Reference: Sahih Ibn Majah 2/321

English

## 43 PRAYER FOR FORGIVENESS (3)

رَبَّنَآ ءَامَنَّا فَٱغْفِرْ لَنَا وَٱرْحَمْنَا وَأَنتَ خَيْرُ ٱلرَّٰحِمِينَ.

Arabic

Rabbana amanna, faghfir lana warhamna, wa anta khayru rahimeena.

Phonetic transcription

Reference: Surat Al-Mu'minun (23:109)

Our Lord, we have believed, so forgive us and have mercy upon us, and You are the Most Merciful.

English

## 44 PRAYER FOR FORGIVENESS (4)

رَّبِّ ٱغْفِرْ وَٱرْحَمْ وَأَنتَ خَيْرُ ٱلرَّٰحِمِينَ.

Arabic

Rabbi ghfir warham wa Anta khairur raahimeen.

Phonetic transcription

Reference: Surat Al-Mu'minun (23:118)

O My Lord, forgive and have mercy, for You are the Most Merciful.

English

## 45 PRAYER FOR FORGIVENESS (5)

اللَّهُمَّ إِنَّكَ عَفُوٌّ كَرِيمٌ تُحِبُّ الْعَفْوَ فَاعْفُ عَنِّي.

Arabic

Allahumma innaka 'afuwun, tuhibbu l-'afwa, fa'fu 'anni.

Phonetic transcription

Reference: Riyad as-Salihin 1195

O Allah, You are Most Forgiving, and You love forgiveness; so forgive me.

English

## 46 PRAYER FOR FORGIVENESS (6)

رَبَّنَآ إِنَّنَآ ءَامَنَّا فَٱغْفِرْ لَنَا ذُنُوبَنَا وَقِنَا عَذَابَ ٱلنَّارِ.

Arabic

Rabbana inana amana faghfir lanaa dunubanaa wa qinaa 'adaaban Naari.

Phonetic transcription

Reference: Surat Al Imran (3:16)

Our Lord, indeed we have believed, so forgive us our sins and protect us from the punishment of Hell.

English

## 47 PRAYER FOR FORGIVENESS (7)

لَّآ إِلَٰهَ إِلَّآ أَنتَ سُبْحَٰنَكَ إِنِّي كُنتُ مِنَ ٱلظَّٰلِمِينَ.

Arabic

La ilaha illa anta subhanaka innee kuntu mina aldalimeena.

Phonetic transcription

Reference: Surat Al-Anbiya (21:87)

There is no god but You; Glory be to You. Indeed, I have been among the wrongdoers.

English

## 48 PRAYER FOR FORGIVENESS AND MERCY

اللَّهُمَّ إِنِّي أَسْأَلُكَ بِرَحْمَتِكَ الَّتِي وَسِعَتْ كُلَّ شَيْءٍ أَنْ تَغْفِرَلِي.

Arabic

Allāhumma innī as'aluka bi raḥmatika 'l-latī wasi`at kulla shay' an taghfira lī.

Phonetic transcription

Reference: Ibn Majah 1/557

O Allah, I ask You by Your mercy that encompasses all things to forgive me

English

# 49 PRAYER FOR FORGIVENESS FOR ONESELF, PARENTS AND THE BELIEVERS

رَبَّنَا ٱغۡفِرۡ لِي وَلِوَٰلِدَيَّ وَلِلۡمُؤۡمِنِينَ يَوۡمَ يَقُومُ ٱلۡحِسَابُ.

Arabic

Rabbana ighfir lee wa liwalidaya walilmumineena yawma yaqoomu alhisabu.

Phonetic transcription

Reference Surat Ibrahim (14:41)

O Allah, forgive me and my parents and the believers on the Day of Judgment.

English

# Prayers for protection

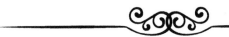

## 50 PRAYER FOR PROTECTION FROM SINS AND FOR FORGIVENESS

اللَّهُمَّ إِنِّي أَعُوذُ بِكَ مِنَ الكَسَلِ وَالهَرَمِ، وَالمَأْثَمِ وَالمَغْرَمِ، وَمِنْ فِتْنَةِ القَبْرِ، وَعَذَابِ القَبْرِ، وَمِنْ فِتْنَةِ النَّارِ وَعَذَابِ النَّارِ، وَمِنْ شَرِّ فِتْنَةِ الغِنَى، وَأَعُوذُ بِكَ مِنْ فِتْنَةِ الفَقْرِ، وَأَعُوذُ بِكَ مِنْ فِتْنَةِ المَسِيحِ الدَّجَّالِ، اللَّهُمَّ اغْسِلْ عَنِّي خَطَايَايَ بِمَاءِ الثَّلْجِ وَالبَرَدِ، وَنَقِّ قَلْبِي مِنَ الخَطَايَا كَمَا نَقَّيْتَ الثَّوْبَ الأَبْيَضَ مِنَ الدَّنَسِ، وَبَاعِدْ بَيْنِي وَبَيْنَ خَطَايَايَ كَمَا بَاعَدْتَ بَيْنَ المَشْرِقِ وَالمَغْرِبِ!

Arabic

Allahumma inni a'udhu bika min al-kasal wal-harami, wal-ma'thami wal-maghrami, wa min fitnati lqabri, wa 'adhabi lqabri, wa min fitnati nari wa 'adhabi nari, wa min sharri fitnati lghina, wa a'udhu bika min fitnati lfaqri, wa a'udhu bika min fitnati lmasihi dajjal. Allahumma ighsil 'anni khataaya bima'i thalji wal-baradi, wa naqqi qalbi mina lkhataaya kama naqqaita thawba l-abyada mina danasi, wa baid bayni wa bayna khataaya kama baidta bayna lmashriqi wa lmaghrib.

Phonetic transcription

Reference: Jami` at-Tirmidhi 3495

O Allah, I seek refuge in You from laziness and old age, from sins and debts, and from the turmoil and punishment of the grave. I seek refuge in You from the trials and punishment of Hell, and from the evil trials of wealth. I seek refuge in You from the turmoils of poverty, and I seek refuge in You from the temptation of the Antichrist. O Allah, wash away my sins from me with water of ice and hail, and purify my heart from sins as a white garment is purified from filth. Create a great distance between me and my sins as You have created East and West.

English

## 51 PRAYER FOR PROTECTION FROM WEAKNESSES OF CHARACTER

اللَهُمَّ إِنِّي أعُوذُ بِكَ مِنَ البُخْلِ، وَأَعوذُ بِكَ مِنَ الجُبْنِ، وَأعوذُ بِكَ أنْ أُرَدَّ إِلَى أَرْذَلِ العُمُرِ، وَأعُوذُ بِكَ مِنْ فِتْنَةِ الدُّنْيَا، وَأَعُوذُ بِكَ مِنْ عَذَابِ القَبْرِ.

Arabic

Allahumma inni a'udhu bika min al-bukhli, wa a'udhu bika min al-jubni, wa a'udhu bika an arudda ila arzalil 'umur, wa a'udhu bika min fitnatid-dunya, ya'ni fitnatid-dajjal, wa a'udhu bika min 'adhabil-qabr.

Phonetic transcription

Reference: Al-Bukhari, cf. Al-Asqalani, Fathul-Bari 6/35

O Allah, I seek refuge in You from stinginess, cowardice, and from returning to the worst stages of life. I seek refuge in You from the temptations of this world, meaning the temptations of the Antichrist, and I seek refuge in You from the punishment of the grave.

English

## 52 PRAYER FOR PROTECTION FROM THE DIFFICULTIES OF LIFE

اللَّهُمَّ إِنِّي أَعُوذُ بِكَ مِنْ عَذَابِ الْقَبْرِ وَ بِكَ مِنْ فِتْنَةِ الْمَسِيحِ الدَّجَّالِ وَ بِكَ مِنْ فِتْنَةِ الْمَحْيَا وَالْمَمَاتِ اللَّهُمَّ إِنِّي بِكَ مِنَ الْمَأْثَمِ وَالْمَغْرَمِ.

Arabic

Allahumma inni a'udhu bika min 'adhabil-qabr, wa a'udhu bika min fitnatil-masihid-dajjal, wa a'udhu bika min fitnatil-mahya wal-mamat. Allahumma inni a'udhu bika minal-ma'thami wal-maghrami.

Phonetic transcription

Reference: Al-Bukhari 1/202, Muslim 1/412

O Allah, I seek refuge in You from the punishment of the grave, and I seek refuge in You from the trial of the False Messiah, and I seek refuge in You from the trials of life and death. O Allah, I seek refuge in You from sin and from debt.

English

## 53 PRAYER FOR PROTECTION FROM TEMPTATIONS AND TRIALS

اللَّهُمَّ إِنِّي أَعُوذُ بِكَ مِنْ فِتْنَةِ النَّارِ وَمِنْ عَذَابِ النَّارِ، وَأَعُوذُ بِكَ مِنْ فِتْنَةِ الْقَبْرِ، وَأَعُوذُ بِكَ مِنْ عَذَابِ الْقَبْرِ، وَأَعُوذُ بِكَ مِنْ فِتْنَةِ الغِنَى، وَأَعُوذُ بِكَ مِنْ فِتْنَةِ الفَقْرِ، وَأَعُوذُ بِكَ مِنْ فِتْنَةِ المَسِيحِ الدَّجَّالِ.

Arabic

Allahumma, inni a'udhu bika min fitnati nari wa min 'adhabi nari, wa a'udhu bika min fitnati lqabri, wa a'udhu bika min 'adhabi lqabri, wa a'udhu bika min fitnati lghina, wa a'udhu bika min fitnati lfaqri, wa a'udhu bika min fitnati lmasihi dajjal.

Phonetic transcription

O Allah, I seek refuge in You from the turmoils of the Hell and the punishment of the Fire. I seek refuge in You from the turmoils of the grave and the punishment of the grave. I seek refuge in You from the temptations of wealth and the turmoils of poverty. I seek refuge in You from the trials of the Antichrist.

English

Reference: Jami' at-Tirmidhi 3495

## 54 PRAYER FOR PROTECTION FROM FALSE GODS

اللَّهُمَّ إِنِّي أَعُوذُ بِكَ أَنْ أُشْرِكَ بِكَ وَأَنَا أَعْلَمُ، وَأَسْتَغْفِرُكَ لِمَا أَعْلَمُ.

Arabic

Allāhumma innī a`ūdhu bika an ushrika bika wa anā a`lam, wa astaghfiruka limā lā a`lam.

Phonetic transcription

O Allah, I seek refuge in You from associating partners with You while I know, and I seek Your forgiveness for what I do not know.

English

Reference: Ahmad 4/403

## 55 PRAYER FOR THE PROTECTION OF THE HUMAN SOUL

بِسْمِ اللَّهِ أَرْقِيكَ مِنْ كُلِّ شَيْءٍ يُؤْذِيكَ مِنْ شرك كُلِّ نَفْسٍ أَوْ عَيْنِ حَاسِدٍ اللَّهُ يَشْفِيكَ بِسم الله أرقيك.

Arabic

Bismillah, arqiika min kulli shay'in yu'dhika, min sharri kulli nafsin aw 'ayn hasidin. Allah yashfeek. Bismillah, arqiika.

Phonetic transcription

In the name of Allah, I invoke for You, seeking protection from every harm, protecting You from the evil of every envious soul or eye. May Allah heal You; I invoke for You in the name of Allah.

English

Reference: Sahih Muslim 2186

# 56 PRAYER FOR THE PROTECTION FROM THE EVIL EYE

وَلَوْلَا إِذْ دَخَلْتَ جَنَّتَكَ قُلْتَ مَا شَاءَ اللَّهُ لَا قُوَّةَ إِلَّا بِاللَّهِ.

Arabic

Walawla id dakhalta jannataka qulta ma shaa lahu la quwata illa billahi.

Phonetic transcription

Reference: Surat Kahf (18.39)

What if when You entered Your garden and said "What Allah willed has occurred; there is no power except in Allah".

English

# 57 PRAYER FOR THE PROTECTION FROM THE DEVIL AND HIS TEMPTATIONS

أَعُوذُ بِاللَّهِ مِنَ الشَّيطَانِ الرَّجِيمِ.

Arabic

A'udhu billahi min ash-shaytan ir-rajim.

Phonetic transcription

Reference: Al-Bukhari 7/99, Muslim 4/2015

I seek refuge in Allah from the accursed Satan.

English

# 58 PRAYER FOR THE PROTECTION FROM GOD'S WRATH

اللَّهُمَّ إِنِّي أَعُوذُ بِكَ مِنْ زَوَالِ نِعْمَتِكَ، وَتَحَوُّلِ عَافِيَتِكَ، وَفُجَاءَةِ نِقْمَتِكَ، وَجَمِيعِ سَخَطِكَ.

Arabic

Allahumma inni a'udhu bika min zawali ni'matika, wa tahawwuli 'afiyatika, wa fuja'ati niqmatika, wa jami'i sakhatika.

Phonetic transcription

Reference: Riyad as-Salihin 1478

O Allah! I seek refuge in You against the declining of Your Favours, the change of Your protection, the suddenness of Your punishment and all that which displeases You.

English

## 59 PRAYER FOR SEEKING REFUGE IN ALLAH

أَعُوذُ بِعِزَّتِكَ الَّذِي لَا إِلَهَ إِلَّا أَنْتَ الَّذِي لَا يَمُوتُ وَالْجِنُّ وَالْإِنْسُ يَمُوتُونَ.

Arabic

Allahumma inni a'oodhu bi'izzatika la ilaha illa anta an tudillani anta lhayu ladhi la yamootu wa ljinnu wa linsu yamootoon.

O Allah, I seek refuge in Your might. There is no god but You. Protect me from going astray. You are the Ever-Living, who never dies, while the jinn and humans will die.

Phonetic transcription

Reference: Sahih Muslim 2717

English

## 60 PRAYER FOR THE PROTECTION FROM INAPPROPRIATE KNOWLEDGE

رَبِّ إِنِّي أَعُوذُ بِكَ أَنْ أَسْأَلَكَ مَا لَيْسَ لِي بِهِ عِلْمٌ ۖ وَإِلَّا تَغْفِرْ لِي وَتَرْحَمْنِي أَكُن مِّنَ الْخَاسِرِينَ.

Arabic

Rabbi inni a'oodhu bika an as'alaka ma laysa li bihi ilm, wa illa taghfirli wa tarhamni akun mina al-khasireen.

O Allah, I seek refuge in You from asking You about what I have no knowledge of, and unless You forgive me and have mercy on me, I will be among the losers.

Phonetic transcription

Reference: Surat HUD (11:47)

English

## 61 PRAYER FOR THE PROTECTION FROM EVIL ACTS

اللَّهُمَّ إِنِّي أَعُوذُ بِكَ مِنْ شَرِّ مَا عَمِلْتُ وَمِنْ شَرِّ مَا لَمْ أَعْمَلْ.

Arabic

Allahumma, inni a'udhu bika min sharri ma 'amiltu wa min sharri ma lam a'mal.

O Allah, I seek refuge in Thee from the evil of what I have done and from the evil of what I have not done.

Phonetic transcription

Reference: Mishkat al-Masabih 2462

English

## 62 PRAYER FOR THE PROTECTION FROM POVERTY, HARDSHIP AND TYRANNY

اللَّهُمَّ إِنِّي أَعُوذُ بِكَ مِنَ الْفَقْرِ وَالْقِلَّةِ وَالذِّلَّةِ وَأَعُوذُ بِكَ مِنْ أَنْ أَظْلِمَ أَوْ أُظْلَمَ.

Arabic

Allahumma, inni a'udhu bika minal-faqri wa a'udhu bika min al-qillati waddillati, wa a'udhu bika an adlima aw udlam.

Phonetic transcription

Reference: Sunan Abi Dawud 1544

O Allah, I seek refuge in You from poverty, scarcity, and humiliation. I seek refuge in You from oppressing others or being oppressed

English

## 63 PRAYER FOR THE PROTECTION FROM PUNISHMENT OF HELL

رَبَّنَا ٱصْرِفْ عَنَّا عَذَابَ جَهَنَّمَ إِنَّ عَذَابَهَا كَانَ غَرَامًا، إِنَّهَا سَاءَتْ مُسْتَقَرًّا وَمُقَامًا.

Arabic

Rabbana ṣrif 'anna 'adhāba jahannama, inna 'adhābaha kāna ġarāma, innaha sa'at mustaqarran wa muqamā.

Phonetic transcription

Reference: Surat (al-furqan) 25:65-66

O Allah, avert from us the punishment of Hell. Indeed, its punishment is ever adhering; indeed, it is evil as a settlement and residence.

English

## 64 PRAYER FOR THE PROTECTION FROM HUNGER AND BETRAYAL

اللَّهُمَّ إِنِّي أَعُوذُ بِكَ مِنَ الْجُوعِ فَإِنَّهُ بِئْسَ الضَّجِيعُ وَأَعُوذُ بِكَ مِنَ الْخِيَانَةِ فَإِنَّهَا بِئْسَتِ الْبِطَانَةُ.

Arabic

Allahumma inni a'udhu bika minal-ju'l, fa innahu bi'sad-daji'u, wa a'udhu bika minal-khiyanati, fa innahu bi'satil-bitanah.

Phonetic transcription

Reference: Sunan an-Nasa'i 5468

O Allah, I seek refuge in You from hunger, for it is an evil bedfellow; and I seek refuge in You from treachery, for it is an evil companion.

English

## 65 PRAYER FOR THE PROTECTION FROM OUR FELLOW HUMAN BEINGS

اللَّهُمَّ إِنَّا نجعلُكَ في نحورِهِمْ، ونعُوذُ بِكَ مِنْ شرُورِهِمْ.

Arabic

Allahumma inna naj'aluka fee nuhurihim, wa na'oodhu bika min shururihim.

O Allah, we ask You to restrain them by their necks, and we seek refuge in You from their evil.

Reference: Abu Dawud 2/89

Phonetic transcription

English

## 66 PRAYER FOR THE PROTECTION FROM A BAD LEADER

اللهُ أَكْبَرُ، اللَّهُ أَعَزُّ مِنْ خَلْقِهِ جَمِيعًا، اللَّهُ أَعَزُّ مِمَّا أَخَافُ وَأَحْذَرُ، وَأَعُوذُ بِاللَّهِ الَّذِي لا إِلَهَ إِلا هُوَ، الْمُمْسِكُ
السَّمَاوَاتِ السَّبْعَ أَنْ يَقَعْنَ عَلَى الأَرْضِ إِلا بِإِذْنِهِ، مِنْ شَرِّ عَبْدِكَ فُلانٍ، وَجُنُودِهِ وَأَتْبَاعِهِ وَأَشْيَاعِهِ مِنَ الْجِنِّ
وَالإِنْسِ، اللَّهُمَّ كُنْ لِي جَارًا مِنْ شَرِّهِمْ، جَلَّ ثَنَاؤُكَ، وَعَزَّ جَارُكَ، وَتَبَارَكَ اسْمُكَ، وَلا إِلَهَ غَيْرُكَ.

Arabic

Allahu Akbar, Allahu A'azzu min khalkihi jamee'an, Allahu A'azzu mimma akhafu wa ahdharu, wa a'oodhu billahi allathi la ilaha illa huwa, al-mumisiku as-samaawati as-sab'a an yaqa'unna 'ala al-ardi illa bi-idhnihi, min sharri 'abdika fulanin, wa junoodihi wa atbaa'ihi wa ashyaihi min al-jinni wal-insi. Allahumma kun li jaaran min sharrihim, jal thana'uka, wa 'azza jaaruka, wa tabarak ismuka, wa la ilaha ghayruka.

Allah is greater. Allah is mightier than all His creation and Allah is greater than all that I fear and beware. I seek refuge with Allah. There is no god but Him, the One who keeps the seven heavens from falling onto the earth by nothing except His permission, from the evil of Your servant (name of the person) and his armies and followers and supporters, both among jinn and men. O Allah, be my protector against their evil. Your praise is great and Your protection is immense, Blessed is Your Name. There is no god but You.

Reference: Al-Adab Al-Mufrad 708

Phonetic transcription

English

## 67 PRAYER FOR THE PROTECTION FROM ALL KINDS OF DANGERS

اللَّهُمَّ إِنِّي أَعُوذُ بِكَ مِنَ الْهَدْمِ وَأَعُوذُ بِكَ مِنَ التَّرَدِّي وَأَعُوذُ بِكَ مِنَ الْغَرَقِ وَالْحَرَقِ وَالْهَرَمِ وَأَعُوذُ بِكَ
أَنْ يَتَخَبَّطَنِي الشَّيْطَانُ عِنْدَ الْمَوْتِ وَأَعُوذُ بِكَ أَنْ أَمُوتَ فِي سَبِيلِكَ مُدْبِرًا وَأَعُوذُ بِكَ أَنْ أَمُوتَ لَدِيغًا.

Arabic

Allahumma inni a'udhu bika minal-hadmi, wa a'udhu bika minat-taraddi, wa a'udhu bika minal-gharaqi, wal-hariqi, wa a'udhu bika an yatakhabbatanish-shaitanu 'indal-mawti, wa a'udhu bika an amuta fi sabilika mudbiran, wa a'udhu bika an amuta ladigha.

O Allah, I seek refuge in You from ruin, I seek refuge in You from degradation, I seek refuge in You from drowning, burning, and and senility. I seek refuge in You from being tempted by Satan at the time of death, and I seek refuge in You from dying while fleeing. I seek refuge in You from a venomous sting.

Reference: Sunan an-Nasa'i 5533

Phonetic transcription

English

## 68 PRAYER FOR THE PROTECTION FROM DANGERS ON THE JOURNEYS

اللهُمَّ إِنَّا نَسْأَلُكَ فِي سَفَرِنَا هَذَا الْبِرَّا وَالتَّقْوَى، وَمِنَ الْعَمَلِ مَا تَرْضَى، اللهُمَّ هَوِّنْ عَلَيْنَا سَفَرَنَا هَذَا،
وَاطْوِ عَنَّا بُعْدَهُ، اللهُمَّ أَنْتَ الصَّاحِبُ فِي السَّفَرِ، وَالْخَلِيفَةُ فِي الأَهْلِ، اللهُمَّ إِنِّي أَعُوذُ بِكَ مِنْ وَعْثَاءِ
السَّفَرِ، وَكَآبَةِ الْمَنْظَرِ، وَسُوءِ الْمُنْقَلَبِ فِي الْمَالِ وَالأَهْلِ.

Arabic

Allahumma, inna nas'aluka fi safarina hadha al-birra wa at-taqwa, wa min al-'amali ma tarda, Allahumma hawwin 'alayna safarana hadha, wa atwi 'anna bu'dahu, Allahumma anta as-sahibu fi as-safari, wal-khalifatu fi al-ahli, Allahumma inni a'oodhu bika min wa'tha'i safari, wa kaaba-ti al-manzari, wa su'i al-munqalabi fi al-mali wal-ahl.

Phonetic transcription

Reference: Muslim 2/978

O Allah, we ask You for righteousness and piety during this journey, and for deeds that please You. O Allah, make this journey easy for us, and shorten its distance for us. O Allah, You are our companion during the journey, and the successor over our family. O Allah, I seek refuge in You from the difficulties of travel, from having a gloomy sight, and from a bad return in my wealth and family.

English

## 69 PRAYER FOR THE PROTECTION FROM THE DEVIL AND FORNICATION

بِسْمِ اللهِ اللَّهُمَّ جَنِّبْنَا الشَّيْطَانَ وَجَنِّبْ الشَّيْطَانَ مَا رَزَقْتَنَا!

Arabic

Bismillāh. Allāhumma jannibna Shayṭān, wa jannibi Shayṭāna mā razaqtanā.

Phonetic transcription

Reference: Al-Bukhari 6/141, Muslim 2/1028

In the name of Allah. O Allah, keep us away from Satan and keep Satan away from what You have blessed us with.

English

## 70 PRAYER FOR THE PROTECTION FROM MANY DANGERS

اللَّهُمَّ اكْفِنِيهِم بِمَا شِئْتَ.

Arabic

Allahumma kfini-him bima shi't.

Phonetic transcription

Reference: Muslim 4/2300

O Allah, suffice me against them in any way You will.

English

# 71 PRAYER FOR THE PROTECTION FROM HOSTILE PEOPLE

اللَّهُمَّ إِنَّا نَجْعَلُكَ فِي نُحُورِهِمْ، وَنَعُوذُ بِكَ مِنْ شُرُورِهِمْ.



Arabic

Allahumma inna naj'aluka fee nuhurihim, wa na'oodhu bika min shururihim.

O Allah, we ask You to restrain them by their necks, and we seek refuge in You from their evil.

Phonetic transcription

Reference: Abu Dawud 2/89

English

---

# 72 PRAYER FOR THE PROTECTION FROM BLASPHEMY AND IDOLATRY

اللَّهُمَّ إِنِّي أَعُوذُ بِكَ أَنْ أُشْرِكَ بِكَ وَأَنَا أَعْلَمُ وَأَسْتَغْفِرُكَ لِمَا أَعْلَمُ.



Arabic

Allahumma inni a'oodhu bika an ushrika bika wa ana a'lamu wa astaghfiruka lima la a'lamu.

O Allah, I seek refuge in You from associating partners with You while I know, and I seek Your forgiveness for what I do not know.

Phonetic transcription

Reference: Ahmad 4/403

English

---

# 73 PRAYER FOR THE PROTECTION FROM JEALOUSY AND PRYING EYES

بِسْمِ اللَّهِ أَرْقِي نَفْسِي، مِنْ كُلِّ شَيْءٍ يُؤْذِينِي مِنْ شَرِّ كُلِّ نَفْسٍ أَوْ عَيْنٍ حَاسِدٍ اللَّهُ يَشْفِينِي، بِسْمِ اللَّهِ أَرْقِي نَفْسِي.



Arabic

Bismillah arqi nafsi, min kulli shay'in yu'dheeni, wa min sharri kulli nafsin aw 'aynin hasid, Allah yashfeeni, bismillah arqi nafsi.

In the name of Allah, I purify myself from everything that harms me, and from the evil of every soul or envious eye. May God heal me. In the name of God, I purify myself.

Phonetic transcription

Reference: Sahih Muslim

English

## 74 PRAYER FOR THE PROTECTION FROM THE DEVIL AND THE EVIL EYE

أُعِيذُكُمَا بِكَلِمَاتِ اللهِ التَّامَّةِ مِنْ كُلِّ شَيْطَانٍ وَ هَامَّةٍ وَمِنْ كُلِّ عَيْنٍ لاَمَّةٍ.

Arabic

U'idhukuma bikalimati llahi tammati,min kulli shaitanin wa hammatin, wa minkulli 'aynin lammah.

I seek refuge for You both in the perfect words of Allah from every devil, harmful creature, and evil eye.

Phonetic transcription

Reference: Jami' at-Tirmidhi 2060

English

## 75 PRAYER FOR THE PROTECTION FROM DECEITFUL PEOPLE

اللَّهُمَّ احْفَظْنِي مِنْ بَيْنِ يَدَىَّ وَمِنْ خَلْفِي وَ عَنْ يَمِينِي وَ عَنْ شِمَالِي وَمِنْ فَوْقِي وَ أَعُوذُ بِعَظَمَتِكَ أُغْتَالَ مِنْ تَحْتِيِي.

Arabic

Allahumma ihfazni min bayni yadayya wa min khalfi wa'an yameeni wa'an shimali wa min fawqi. Wa a'oodhu bia'zamatika an ughatala min tahti.

O Allah, protect me from in front, from behind, from my right, from my left, and from above. I seek refuge in Your greatness from being seized from beneath.

Phonetic transcription

Reference: Sahih Ibn Majah 2/332 and Abu Dawud

English

## 76 PRAYER FOR MERCY, SUSTENANCE AND PROTECTION

اللَّهُمَّ اغْفِرْ لِي، وَارْحَمْنِي، وَاهْدِنِي، وَعَافِنِي، وَارْزُقْنِي.

Arabic

Allahumma, ighfir li, warhamni, wahdini, wa'afini, warzuqni.

O Allah, forgive me, have mercy on me, guide me, protect my health, and grant me provision.

Phonetic transcription

Reference: Abu Dawud, Ibn Majah, At-Tirmidhi

English

## 77 PRAYER FOR THE PROTECTION FROM IRRESPONSIBLE ACTS

اللَّهُمَّ إِنِّي أَعُوذُ بِكَ أَنْ أَضِلَّ أَوْ أُضَلَّ أَوْ أَزِلَّ أَوْ أُزَلَّ أَوْ أَظْلِمَ أَوْ أُظْلَمَ أَوْ أَجْهَلَ أَوْ يُجْهَلَ عَلَيَّ.

Arabic

Allahumma inni a'oodhu bika an adhilla aw udhalla, aw azilla aw uzalla, aw athlima aw uthlama, aw ajhala aw yujhala 'alayya.

O Allah, I seek refuge in You from going astray or leading others astray, slipping or causing others to slip, wronging or being wronged, and from acting in ignorance or being treated ignorantly towards me.

Phonetic transcription

Reference: Abu Dawud, Ibn Majah, An-Nasa'i, At-Tirmidhi

English

## 78 PRAYER FOR THE PROTECTION FROM EVIL

أَعُوذُ بِكَلِمَاتِ اللهِ التَّامَّةِ مِنْ شَرِّ مَا خَلَقَ.

Arabic

A'oodhu bikalimati llahi at-tammati min sharri ma khalaqa.

I seek refuge in the Perfect Words of Allah from the evil of what He has created.

Phonetic transcription

Reference: Muslim 4/2080

English

## 79 PRAYER FOR THE PROTECTION FROM UNFORESEEABLE EVENTS & STRANGERS

اللَّهُمَّ إِنِّي أَسْأَلُكَ خَيْرَهَا وَخَيْرَ مَا جَبَلْتَهَا عَلَيْهِ وَأَعُوذُ بِكَ مِنْ شَرِّهَا وَمِنْ شَرِّ مَا جَبَلْتَهَا عَلَيْهِ.

Arabic

Allāhumma innī as'aluka khayrahā wa khayra mā jabaltahā `alayh, wa a`ūdhu bika min sharrihā.

O Allah, I ask You for its goodness, and the goodness upon which You have created it, and I seek refuge in You from its evil.

Phonetic transcription

Reference: Abu Dawud 2/248 and Ibn Majah 1/617

English

## 80 PRAYER FOR THE PROTECTION FROM EVIL

أعوذُ بِكَلِماتِ اللهِ التّامّاتِ مِنْ شَرِّ ما خَلَق.

Arabic

A'oodhu bikalimatillahi at-tammati min sharri ma khalaqa.

I seek refuge in the Perfect Words of Allah from the evil of what He has created.

Reference: Muslim 4/2080

Phonetic transcription

English

## 81 PRAYER FOR PROTECTION WHILE SLEEPING

أَمْسَيْنَا وَأَمْسَى الْمُلْكُ لِلَّهِ. الْحَمْدُ لِلَّهِ، لاَ إِلَهَ إِلاَّ اللَّهُ وَحْدَهُ لاَ شَرِيكَ لَهُ الْمُلْكُ وَلَهُ الْحَمْدُ وَهُوَ عَلَى كُلِّ
شَيْءٍ قَدِيرٌ رَبِّ أَسْأَلُكَ خَيْرَ مَا فِي هَذِهِ اللَّيْلَةِ وَخَيْرَ مَا بَعْدَهَا وَأَعُوذُ بِكَ مِنْ شَرِّ مَا فِي هَذِهِ اللَّيْلَةِ
وَشَرِّ مَا بَعْدَهَا رَبِّ أَعُوذُ بِكَ مِنَ الْكَسَلِ وَمِنْ سُوءِ الْكِبْرِ أَوِ الْكُفْرِ رَبِّ أَعُوذُ بِكَ مِنْ عَذَابٍ فِي النَّارِ
وَعَذَابٍ فِي الْقَبْرِ.

Arabic

Amsaynaa wa amsa lmulkoo lillahi. Al-hamdu lillah, laa ilaha illa llah wahdahu laa shareeka lah. Lahu lmulku wa lahu lhamdu wa huwa 'ala kulli shayin qadeer. Rabbi as'aluka khaira ma fee hadhihi laylah wa khaira ma ba'daha. Wa a'oodhu bika min sharri ma fee hadhihi laylah wa sharri ma ba'daha. Rabbi a'oodhu bika mina lkasali wa min soo'i lkibri awi lkufri. Rabbi a'oodhu bika min 'adabin fi nnar wa 'adabin fi lqabr.

We have entered a new evening, and all dominion belongs to Allah. Praise be to Allah. There is no god but Allah, alone, without any partner. To Him belongs all sovereignty and praise, and He is omnipotent over all things. O Allah, I ask You for the good of this night and the good that follows it. I seek refuge in You from the evil of this night and the evil that follows it. O Allah, I seek refuge in You from laziness and the evil of arrogance or disbelief. O Allah, I seek refuge in You from the torment of the Hell and the torment of the grave.

Reference: Jami' at-Tirmidhi 3390

Phonetic transcription

English

## 82 PRAYER FOR THE FOR PROTECTION FROM THE DEVIL

رَّبِّ أَعُوذُ بِكَ مِنْ هَمَزَٰتِ ٱلشَّيَٰطِينِ. وَأَعُوذُ بِكَ رَبِّ أَن يَحْضُرُونِ.

Arabic

Rabbi a'oodhu bika min hamazati shayateen, wa a'oodhu bika Rabbi an yahdhuroon.

O Allah, I seek refuge in You from the incitements of the devils, and I seek refuge in You, my Lord, that they be present.

Reference: Abu Dawud 4/12

Phonetic transcription

English

## 83 PRAYER FOR THE FOR PROTECTION FROM IGNORANCE

أَعُوذُ بِٱللَّهِ أَنْ أَكُونَ مِنَ ٱلْجَٰهِلِينَ.

Arabic

A'oodhu billahi an akoona min al-jahileen.

I seek refuge in Allah from being among the ignorant.

Phonetic transcription

Reference: Surat (al-Baqara) 2:67

English

## 84 PRAYER FOR THE FOR FOR DEFENSE AGAINST THE TRICKS OF THE REBELLIOUS DEVIL

أعُوذُ بِكَلِمَاتِ اللهِ التَّامَّاتِ الَّتِي لا يُجَاوِزُهُنَّ بَرّ وَلَا فَاجِرٌ مِنْ شَرِّ مَا خَلَقَ، وَبَرَأَ وَذَرأَ، وَمِنْ شَرِّ مَا
يَنْزِلُ مِنَ السَّمَاءِ، وَمِنْ شَرِّ مَا يَعْرُجُ فِيهَا، وَمِنْ شَرِّ مَا ذَرَأَ فِي الْأَرْضِ، وَمِنْ شَرِّ مَا يَخْرُجُ مِنْهَا،
وَمِنْ شَرِّ فِتَنِ اللَّيْلِ وَالنَّهَارِ، وَمِنْ شَرِّ كُلِّ طَارِقٍ إِلَّا طَارِقاً يَطْرُقُ بِخَيْرٍ يَا رَحْمَنُ.

Arabic

A'oodhu bikalimatillahi at-tammati allati la yujawizuhunna barrun wala fajirun, min sharri ma khalaqa, wa bara'a wa dara'a, wa min sharri ma yanzilu min as-sama'i wa min sharri ma ya'ruju fiha, wa min sharri ma dara'a fi al-ardi wa min sharri ma yakhruju minha, wa min sharri fitan il-layli wal-nahar, wa min sharri kulli tariqin illa tariqan yatruqu bikhayr, ya Rahman.

I seek refuge in the perfect words of Allah, which no righteous nor wicked person may overcome, from the evil of what He has created, originated, and from the evil of what descends from the sky, and ascends therein. I seek refuge from the evil of what He has created on the earth and comes out of it. I seek refuge from the evil of the temptations of the night and day, of everyone who visits with evil, except for the one who brings good. O Most Merciful.

Phonetic transcription

Reference: Ahmad 3/419

English

# Prayers for support

## 85 PRAYER FOR SUPPORT AND GUIDANCE

رَبِّ أَعِنِّي وَلَا تُعِنْ عَلَيَّ، وَانْصُرْنِي وَلَا تَنْصُرْ عَلَيَّ، وَامْكُرْ لِي وَلَا تَمْكُرْ عَلَيَّ، وَاهْدِنِي وَيَسِّرْ هُدَايَ إِلَيَّ، وَانْصُرْنِي عَلَى مَنْ بَغَى عَلَيَّ، اللَّهُمَّ اجْعَلْنِي لَكَ شَاكِرًا، لَكَ ذَاكِرًا، لَكَ رَاهِبًا، لَكَ مِطْوَاعًا إِلَيْكَ، مُخْبِتًا، أَوْ مُنِيبًا، رَبِّ تَقَبَّلْ تَوْبَتِي، وَاغْسِلْ حَوْبَتِي، وَأَجِبْ دَعْوَتِي، وَثَبِّتْ حُجَّتِي، وَاهْدِ قَلْبِي، وَسَدِّدْ لِسَانِي، وَاسْلُلْ سَخِيمَةَ قَلْبِي.

Arabic

Rabbi a'inni wala tu'in 'alayya, wansurni wala tansur 'alayya, wamkur li wala tamkur 'alayya, wahdini wa yassir hudaaya ilayya, wansurni 'alaa man bagha 'alayya. Allahumma ij'alni laka shaakiran, laka zaakiran, laka raahiban, laka muti'an ilayka, mukhbitan aw muniban. Rabbi taqabbal tawbati, wa ghsil hawbati, wa ajib da'wati, wa thabbit hujjati, wahdi qalbi, wasdidd lisaani, waslul sakhiimata qalbi.

Reference: Jami at-Tirmidhi 3551

O Allah, help me and do not help against me, support me and do not support against me, plot for me and do not plot against me, guide me and make my guidance easy for me. Help me against those who transgress against me. O Allah, make me grateful to You, mindful of You, reverent towards You, obedient to You, humble before You, penitent, or constantly turning to You in repentance. O Allah, accept my repentance, wash away my sins, answer my supplication, establish my proof, guide my heart, make my tongue true, and remove the hatred from my heart.

Phonetic transcription

English

## 86 PRAYER FOR MERCY IN THE DIFFICULT TIMES OF LIFE

اللَّهُمَّ رَحْمَتَكَ أَرْجُو فَلاَ تَكِلْنِي إِلَى نَفْسِي طَرْفَةَ عَيْنٍ وَأَصْلِحْ لِي شَأْنِي كُلَّهُ لاَ إِلَهَ إِلاَّ أَنْتَ.

Arabic

Allahumma, rahmataka arju, fala takilni ila nafsi tarfata 'ayn, wa aslih li shani kullahu, la ilaha illa anta.

O Allah, I hope for Your mercy. Do not leave me to myself even for a very short momento and rectify for me all of my affairs. There is no deity worthy of worship except You.

Phonetic transcription

Reference: Abu Dawud 4/324, Ahmad 5/42

English

## 87 PRAYER TO EASE THE SORROW

اللَّهمَّ لا سَهْلَ إلَّا ما جعَلْتَه سَهلًا وأنتَ تجعَلُ الحَزْنَ سَهلًا إذا شِئْتَ.

Arabic

Allahumma, laa sahla illa ma ja'altahu sahlan, wa anta taj'alul hazna sahlan idha shi'ta.

O Allah, there is no ease except in what You have made easy, and You make the difficult easy if You will.

Phonetic transcription

Reference: Ibn Hibban in his Sahih (no. 2427)

English

# 88 PRAYER FOR ADVICE AND HELP

اللَّهُمَّ إنِّي أَسْتَخِيرُكَ بِعِلْمِكَ، وَأَسْتَقْدِرُكَ بِقُدْرَتِكَ، وَأَسْأَلُكَ مِنْ فَضْلِكَ الْعَظِيمِ فَإِنَّكَ تَقْدِرُ وَلا أَقْدِرُ، وَتَعْلَمُ، وَأَنْتَ عَلامُ الْغُيُوبِ.. اللَّهُمَّ إنْ كُنْتَ تَعْلَمُ أَنَّ هَذَا الأَمْرَ خَيْرٌ لِي فِي دِينِي وَمَعَاشِي وَعَاقِبَةِ أَمْرِي؛ فَاقْدُرْهُ لِي وَيَسِّرْهُ لِي ثُمَّ بَارِكْ لِي فِيهِ. اللَّهُمَّ وَإِنْ كُنْتَ تَعْلَمُ أَنَّ هَذَا الأَمْرَشَرٌّ لِي فِي دِينِي وَمَعَاشِي وَعَاقِبَةِ أَمْرِي فَاصْرِفْهُ عَنِّي وَاصْرِفْنِي عَنْهُ وَاقْدُرْ لِي الْخَيْرَ حَيْثُ كَانَ ثُمَّ ارْضِنِي بِهِ.

Arabic

Allahumma, inni astakhiruka biilmika, wa astaqdiruka biqudratika, wa as'aluka min fadlika al-'adim. Fa innaka taqdiru wa la aqdir, wa ta'lamu wa la a'lam, wa anta 'allamu lghuyub. Allahumma, in kunta ta'lamu anna hadha al-amra khairun li fi deeni wa ma'ashi wa 'aqibati amri, faqdirhu li, wa in kunta ta'lamu anna hadha al-amra sharrun li fi deeni wa ma'ashi wa 'aqibati amri, fasrifhu anni wasrifni anhu, wa qdir li al-khaira haythu kana, thumma ardhini bihi.

Reference: Al-Bukhari 7/162 and Aal-'Imran 3: 159

O Allah, I seek Your guidance through Your knowledge, and I seek Your power through Your Omnipotence, and I ask You for Your immense bounty. Indeed, You have the power, and I do not have the power. You have knowledge, and I do not have knowledge. You are the Knower of the unseen. O Allah, if You know that this matter is good for me in my religion, livelihood, and the outcome of my affairs, then ordain it for me and make it easy for me. And if You know that this matter is harmful to me in my religion, livelihood, and the outcome of my affairs, then turn it away from me and turn me away from it. And ordain for me the good wherever it may be and make me content with it.

Phonetic transcription | English

# 89 PRAYER FOR GUIDANCE AFTER WRONGDOING

عَسَىٰٓ أَن يَهْدِيَنِ رَبِّي لِأَقْرَبَ مِنْ هَٰذَا رَشَدًا.

Arabic

Asa an yahdiyani rabbi li-aqraba min hadha rashada.

Reference: Surat (al-Kahf) 18:24

May Allah guide me to a closer path of guidance than this.

Phonetic transcription | English

# 90 PRAYER TO CONFIRM THE TRUTH

رَبِّ ٱحْكُم بِٱلْحَقِّ وَرَبُّنَا ٱلرَّحْمَٰنُ ٱلْمُسْتَعَانُ عَلَىٰ مَا تَصِفُونَ.

Arabic

Rabbi ohkum bi-lhaqqi warabbuna rahmanu almustaanu 'ala ma tasifoona

Reference: Surat Al-Anbya (21:112)

O Allah, judge between us in truth, and Allah is the Most Merciful, the one whose help is sought against what You describe.

Phonetic transcription | English

## 91 PRAYER FOR SUPPORT AGAINST THE ENEMY

اللَّهُمَّ مُنْزِلَ الْكِتَابِ، سَرِيعَ الْحِسَابِ، اهْزِمِ الأَحْزَابَ، اللَّهُمَّ اهْزِمْهُمْ وَزَلْزِلْهُمْ.

Arabic

Allahumma, munzila al-kitab, saree'a al-hisab, ihzimi al-ahzab. Allahumma, ihzimhum wa zalzilhum.

Phonetic transcription

Reference: Muslim 3/1362

O Allah, Revealer of the Book, Swift in taking account, defeat the factions. O Allah, defeat them and shake them.

English

## 92 PRAYER FOR HELP TO PREVAIL IN COMPETITION

اللهم أنت عَضُدِي ونَصِيرِي، بِكَ أَجُولُ، وبِكَ أَصُولُ، وبك أقاتل.

Arabic

Allahumma anta 'adudi wa naseeri, bika a'hool, wa bika asool, wa bika aqatil.

Phonetic transcription

Reference: Abu Dawud 3/42, At-Tirmidhi 5/572

O Allah, You are my supporter and helper. By You, I turn, and by You, I establish, and by You, I combat.

English

## 93 PRAYER FOR JUST PUNISHMENTS FOR WEALTHY SINNERS

رَبَّنَا ٱطْمِسْ عَلَىٰٓ أَمْوَٰلِهِمْ وَٱشْدُدْ عَلَىٰ قُلُوبِهِمْ فَلَا يُؤْمِنُوا۟ حَتَّىٰ يَرَوُا۟ ٱلْعَذَابَ ٱلْأَلِيمَ.

Arabic

Rabbana tmis 'ala amwalihim wa shdud 'ala qulubihim fala yuminu hatta yarawu al-'adhaba al-alim.

Phonetic transcription

Reference: Surat Yunus (10.88)

O Allah, obliterate their wealth and harden their hearts so that they will not believe until they see the painful punishment.

English

## 94 PRAYER FOR HELP IN A CONFLICT SITUATION

اللَّهُمَّ مُنْزِلَ الكِتَابِ، سَرِيعَ الحِسَابِ، اهْزِمِ الأَحْزَابَ، اهْزِمْهُمْ وَزَلْزِلْهُمْ.

Arabic

Allahumma, munzila al-kitab, saree'a al-hisab, ihzimi al-ahzab. Allahumma, ihzimhum wa zalzilhum.

Phonetic transcription

Reference: Muslim 3/1362

O Allah, Revealer of the Book, Swift in taking account, defeat the factions. O Allah, defeat them and shake them.

English

## 95 PRAYER FOR SUPPORT DURING DEPRESSION

اللَّهُمَّ أَحْيِنِي مَا كَانَتِ الْحَيَاةُ خَيْرًا لِي، وَتَوَفَّنِي إِذَا كَانَتِ الْوَفَاةُ خَيْرًا لِي.

Arabic

Allahumma ahyini ma kanaatil-hayatu khayran li, wa tawaffani idha kanaatil-wafatu khayran li.

Phonetic transcription

Reference: Riyad as-Salihin 585

O Allah, grant me life as long as life is good for me, and grant me death when death is good for me.

English

## 96 PRAYER FOR SUPPORT IN FINANCIAL PROBLEMS, SADNESS AND DISTRESS

اللَّهُمَّ إِنِّي أَعُوذُ بِكَ مِنَ الهَمِّ والحَزَنِ، والعَجْزِ والكَسَلِ، والبُخْلِ والجُبْنِ، وضَلَعِ الدَّيْنِ، وغَلَبَةِ الرِّجَالِ.

Arabic

Allahumma inni a'udhu bika min al-hammi wal-huzni wal-'ajzi wal-kasli wal-bukhli wal-jubni wa dhala'id-dayni wa ghalabatir-rijal.

Phonetic transcription

Reference: Al-Bukhari 7/158

O Allah, I seek refuge in You from worry, sorrow, helplessness, laziness, stinginess, cowardice, the burden of debt, and being overpowered by men.

English

## 97 PRAYER FOR SUPPORT DURING BEREAVEMENT

اللّٰهُمَّ لا سَهْلَ إِلّا ما جَعَلْتَهُ سَهلًا، وَأَنْتَ تَجْعَلُ الْحَزَنَذا شِئْتَ سَهلًا.

Arabic

Allahumma la sahla illa ma ja'altahu sahlan, wa anta taj'alul hazna sahlan.

O Allah, there is no ease except in what You have made easy, and if You please You ease sorrow.

Reference: Ibn Hibban in his Sahih (no. 2427)

Phonetic transcription

English

## 98 PRAYER FOR ALLAH'S FAVOR IN STRESSFUL SITUATIONS

اللَّهُمَّ إِنِّي أَسْأَلُكَ مِنْ فَضْلِكَ.

Arabic

Allahumma inni as-aluka min fadlika.

O Allah, I ask You for Your grace.

Reference: Hisn al-Muslim 21

Phonetic transcription

English

## 99 PRAYER FOR SUPPORT AGAINST THE DISBELIEVERS

رَبَّنَا تُؤَاخِذْنَآ إِن نَّسِينَآ أَوْ أَخْطَأْنَا ۚ رَبَّنَا وَلَا تَحْمِلْ عَلَيْنَآ إِصْرًا كَمَا حَمَلْتَهُۥ عَلَى ٱلَّذِينَ مِن قَبْلِنَا ۚ رَبَّنَا وَلَا
تُحَمِّلْنَا مَا لَا طَاقَةَ لَنَا بِهِۦ ۖ وَٱعْفُ عَنَّا وَٱغْفِرْ لَنَا وَٱرْحَمْنَآ ۚ أَنتَ مَوْلَىٰنَا فَٱنصُرْنَا عَلَى ٱلْقَوْمِ ٱلْكَٰفِرِينَ.

Arabic

Rabbana la tu'akhidhna in naseena aw akhta'na. Rabbana wala tahmil alayna isran kama hamaltahu alal-latheena min qablina. Rabbana wala tuhammilna ma la taqata lana bihi, wa'fu anna, waghfir lana, warhamna. Anta mawlana fansurna alal-qawmil kafireen.

O Allah, do not impose blame upon us if we have forgotten or erred. Our Lord, and lay not upon us a burden like that which You laid upon those before us. Our Lord, and burden us not with that which we have no ability to bear. And pardon us, and forgive us, and have mercy upon us. You are our protector, so give us victory over the disbelieving people.

Reference: Surat Al-Baqarah (2:286)

Phonetic transcription

English

## 100 PRAYER FOR SUPPORT AGAINST LIES

رَبَّنَا لَا تُزِغْ قُلُوبَنَا بَعْدَ إِذْ هَدَيْتَنَا وَهَبْ لَنَا مِن لَّدُنكَ رَحْمَةً إِنَّكَ أَنتَ ٱلْوَهَّابُ.

Arabic

Rabbana la tuzigh qulobana ba'da idh hadaytana wa hab lana min ladunka rahmah, innaka anta lwahhab.

Phonetic transcription

O Allah, do not let our hearts deviate after You have guided us, and grant us mercy from Your presence. Indeed, You are the Bestower.

English

Reference: Surat Al Imran (3:8)

## 101 PRAYER FOR OFFSPRING

رَبِّ لَا تَذَرْنِي فَرْدًا وَأَنتَ خَيْرُ ٱلْوَٰرِثِينَ.

Arabic

Rabbi la tatharnee fardan waanta khayru alwaritheena.

Phonetic transcription

O Allah, do not leave me with no heir, and You are the best of inheritors.

English

Reference: Surat Al-Anbiya (21:89)

## 102 PRAYER FOR SUPPORT IN TIMES OF CRISIS

لا إلهَ إلَّا اللهُ العظيمُ الحليمُ، لا إلهَ إلَّا اللهُ ربُّ العرشِ العظيمُ، لا إلهَ إلَّا اللهُ ربُّ السمواتِ السبعِ وربُّ الأرضِ، وربُّ العرشِ الكريمُ.

Arabic

La ilaha illa Allah, al-Azheem al-Haleem. La ilaha illa Allah, Rabbu al-'Arsh al-Azheem. La ilaha illa Allah, Rabbu as-Samawat wa Rabbu al-Ardi wa Rabbu al-'Arsh al-Kareem.

Phonetic transcription

There is no god but Allah, the Almighty, the Most Forbearing. There is no god but Allah, the Lord of the Great Throne. There is no god but Allah, the Lord of the heavens, the Lord of the Earth, and the Lord of the Noble Throne.

English

Reference: Al-Bukhari 8/154, Muslim 4/2092

## 103 PRAYER FOR SUPPORT IN HOPELESS SITUATIONS

رَبِّ إِنِّي لِمَا أَنْزَلْتَ إِلَيَّ مِنْ خَيْرٍ فَقِيرٌ.

Arabic

Rabbī innī limā anzalta ilayya min khayrin faqīr.

My Lord, indeed I am, for whatever good You would send down to me, in need.

Phonetic transcription

Reference: Surat Al-Qasas (28:24)

English

## 104 PRAYER FOR SUPPORT AND HELP

يا حَـيُّ يا قَيّـومُ بِـرَحْمَـتِكِ أَسْتَـغيث، أَصْلِـحْ لي شَـأْنـي كُلَّـه، وَلا تَكِلـني إِلى نَفْسي طَـرْفَةَ عينٍ.

Arabic

Ya Hayyu Ya Qayyum, birahmatika astaghith. Aslih li sha'ni kullahu, wa la takilni ila nafsi tarfata 'ayn.

O Ever-Living One, O Eternal One, by Your mercy I call on You to set right all my affairs. Do not place me in charge of my soul even for the blinking of an eye.

Phonetic transcription

Reference: Sahihut-Targhib wat-Tarhib, 1/273

English

## 105 PRAYER FOR SUPPORT IN DIFFICULT SITUATIONS

أَنِّي مَسَّنِيَ ٱلضُّرُّ وَأَنتَ أَرْحَمُ ٱلرَّٰحِمِينَ.

Arabic

Innee massaniya ddurru wa anta arhamu alrrahimeena.

Indeed, harm has befallen me, and You are the Most Merciful of the Merciful.

Phonetic transcription

Reference: Surat Al-Anbiya (21:83)

English

# Prayers for success

## 106 PRAYER TO SUCCESSFULLY COMPLETE THE EXAM PREPARATION

اللَّهُمَّ افْتَحْ لي أبْوابَ حكمتكَ وانشر عليّ رحمتكَ وامنُن عليّ بالحفظِ والفهمِ سُبْحَانَكَ لَا عِلْمَ لَنَا إِلَّا مَا عَلَّمْتَنَا إِنَّكَ أَنتَ الْعَلِيمُ الْحَكِيمُ.

Arabic

Allahumma iftah 'alaya abwaba hikmatik, wanshur 'alaya rahmatik, wa mnun 'alaya bilhifd wa lfahm. Subhanaka la 'ilma lana illa ma 'allamtana, innaka anta l'aleem lhakeem.

Phonetic transcription

Reference: Sahih Muslim

O Allah, open for me the doors of Your wisedom and display Your mercy upon me, and grant me protection and understanding. Glory be to You, we have no knowledge except what You taught us. Indeed, You are the All-Knowing, the Wise.

English

## 107 PRAYER FOR COURAGE AND STRENGTH BEFORE GIVING A SPEECH

رَبِّ ٱشْرَحْ لِي صَدْرِي وَيَسِّرْ لِيٓ أَمْرِي وَٱحْلُلْ عُقْدَةً مِّن لِّسَانِي يَفْقَهُواْ قَوْلِي.

Arabic

Rabbi ishrah li sadri wa yassir li amri, waahlul 'uqdatan min lisaani yafqahu qawli.

Phonetic transcription

Reference: Surat Taha (20:25-28)

O Allah, open up my heart, ease my task for me, and remove the impediment from my speech so that they may understand my words.

English

## 108 PRAYER FOR SUCCESS IN EXAMS

اللَّهُمَّ لَا سَهْلَ إلاَّ مَا جَعَلْتَهُ سَهْلاً، وأنْتَ تَجْعَلُ الحَزْنَ إذَا شِئْتَ سَهْلاً.

Arabic

Allahumma la sahla illa ma ja'altahu sahla, wa anta taj'alul huzna idha shi'ta sahla.

Phonetic transcription

Reference: Ibn Hibban in his Sahih (no. 2427)

O Allah, there is no ease except in what You have made easy. You can turn sorrow into ease if You will.

English

## 109 PRAYER FOR A SUCCESSFUL LIFE

اللهُمَّ اجْعَلْنَا مُفْلِحِينَ.

Arabic

Allahuma jealna mina lmuflihin.

O Allah, make us among the successful ones.

Reference: Sunan An-Nasai'

Phonetic transcription

English

## 110 PRAYER FOR A FULFILLING AND PROSPEROUS LIFE

اللَّهُمَّ اجْعَلْ خَيْرَ عُمْرِي آخِرَهُ وَخَيْرَ عَمَلِي خَوَاتِمَهُ وَخَيْرَ أَيَّامِي يَوْمَ أَلْقَاكَ.

Arabic

Allahumma ij'al khayra 'umri akhirahu wa khayra 'amali khawatimahu wa khayra ayami yawma alqaak.

O Allah, make the best part of my life its ending, the best of my deeds its conclusion, and the best of my days the day I meet You.

Fuente: Sunan Al Nasai

Phonetic transcription

English

## 111 PRAYER FOR SUCCESS IN THIS WORLD AND IN THE HEREAFTER

رَبَّنَآ ءَاتِنَا فِي ٱلدُّنْيَا حَسَنَةً وَفِي ٱلْآخِرَةِ حَسَنَةً وَقِنَا عَذَابَ ٱلنَّارِ.

Arabic

Rabbana atina fi ddunya hasanah wa fi lakhirati hasanah wa qina 'adhaba an-nar.

O Allah, give us the good of this world and the good of the Hereafter, and save us from the punishment of Hell.

Reference: Surat Al-Baqarah (2.201)

Phonetic transcription

English

## 112 PRAYERS FOR STIMULATION AND SELF-MOTIVATION

رَبِّ أَوْزِعْنِيٓ أَنْ أَشْكُرَ نِعْمَتَكَ ٱلَّتِيٓ أَنْعَمْتَ عَلَيَّ وَعَلَىٰ وَٰلِدَيَّ وَأَنْ أَعْمَلَ صَٰلِحًا تَرْضَىٰهُ وَأَصْلِحْ لِي فِي ذُرِّيَّتِيٓ ۖ إِنِّي تُبْتُ إِلَيْكَ وَإِنِّي مِنَ ٱلْمُسْلِمِينَ.

Arabic

Rabbi awzi'ni an ashkura ni'mataka allati an'amta 'alaya wa 'ala walidaya wa an a'mala salihan tardahu wa aslih li fi dhurriyati. Innī tubtu ilayka wa innī mina l-muslimin.

Phonetic transcription

Reference: Surat Al-Ahqaaf (46:15)

O Allah, enable me to be grateful for Your favour which You have bestowed upon me and upon my parents, and to do righteous deeds that You approve. And make my descendants righteous. Indeed, I repent to You, and indeed, I am among the Muslims.

English

## 113 PRAYER FOR SUCCESS IN THE EXAMS

رَّبِّ أَدْخِلْنِي مُدْخَلَ صِدْقٍ وَأَخْرِجْنِي مُخْرَجَ صِدْقٍ وَٱجْعَل لِّي مِن لَّدُنكَ سُلْطَٰنًا نَّصِيرًا.

Arabic

Rabbi, adkhilni mudkhala sidqin wa akhrijni mukhraja sidqin waj'al li min ladunka sultanan naseera.

Phonetic transcription

Reference: Surat Al-Isra (17:80)

O Allah, admit me in a truthful entrance and let me depart in a truthful departure, and grant me from Yourself a supporting authority.

English

## 114 PRAYER FOR KNOWLEDGE AND ITS PROPER APPLICATION

اللَّهُمَّ انْفَعْنِي بِمَا عَلَّمْتَنِي، وَعَلِّمْنِي مَا يَنْفَعُنِي، وَزِدْنِي عِلْمًا.

Arabic

Allahumm nfa'ni bima 'allamtani, wa 'allimni ma yanfa'uni, wa zidni 'ilma.

Phonetic transcription

Reference: Sunan Ibn Majah 251

O Allah, benefit me by that which You have taught me, and teach me that which will benefit me, and increase my knowledge.

English

## 115 PRAYER FOR A GOOD AND PROSPEROUS LIFE

اللَّهُمَّ أَصْلِحْ لِي دِينِي الَّذِي هُوَ عِصْمَةُ أَمْرِي، وَأَصْلِحْ لِي دُنْيَايَ الَّتِي فِيهَا مَعَاشِي، وَأَصْلِحْ لِي آخِرَتِي الَّتِي إِلَيْهَا مَعَادِي، وَاجْعَلِ الْحَيَاةَ زِيَادَةً لِي فِي كُلِّ خَيْرٍ، وَاجْعَلِ الْمَوْتَ رَاحَةً لِي مِنْ كُلِّ شَرٍّ.

Arabic

Allahumma aslih li deeni allathi huwa 'ismatu amri, wa aslih li dunyaya allati feeha ma'ashi, wa aslih li akhirati allati ilayha ma'adi. Waj'alil-hayata ziyadatan li fi kulli khayr, wa waj'alil-mawta raḥatan li min kulli shar.

Reference: Sahih Muslim Book 17, Hadith 1472

O Allah, rectify my religion which is the safeguard of my affairs, and rectify my worldly life in which is my livelihood, and rectify my Hereafter to which is my return. Make life an increase for me in every goodness, and make death a comfort for me from every evil.

Phonetic transcription

English

## 116 PRAYER FOR A PROSPEROUS DAY

أَصْبَحْنا وَأَصْبَحَ المُلْكُ لله وَالحَمدُ لله، لا إلهَ إلاّ اللّهُ وَحدَهُ لا شَريكَ لهُ، لهُ المُلكُ ولهُ الحَمْد، وهوَ على كلّ شَيءٍ قدير، رَبِّ أسْأَلُكَ خَيرَ ما في هذا اليوم وَخَيرَ ما بَعْدَه، وَأَعوذُ بِكَ مِنْ شَرِّ ما في هذا اليوم وَشَرِّ ما بَعْدَه.

Arabic

Asbahna wa asbaha lmulku lillah, walhamdu lillah. La ilaha illa llahu, wahdahu la sharika lah. Lahu lmulku wa lahu lhamd, wa Huwa 'ala kulli shay'in Qadir. Rabbi as'aluka khaira ma fi hadha al-yawmi, wa khaira ma ba'dahu. Wa a'udhu bika min sharri ma fi hadha al-yawmi, wa sharri ma ba'dahu.

Reference: 3 Muslim 4/2088

We have entered a new day and with it all dominion is Allah's. Praise is to Allah. None has the right to be worshipped but Allah alone, Who has no partner. To Allah belongs the dominion, and to Him is the praise and He is Able to do all things. O Allah, I ask You for the goodness of this day and of the days that come after it, and I seek refuge in You from the evil of this day and of the days that come after it.

Phonetic transcription

English

## 117 PRAYER FOR BUSINESS SUCCESS

اللَّهُمَّ إِنِّي أَسْأَلُكَ عِلْمًا نَافِعًا، وَرِزْقًا طَيِّبًا، وَعَمَلًا مُتَقَبَّلًا.

Arabic

Allahumma inni as'aluka 'ilman nafi'an, wa rizqan tayyiban, wa 'amalan mutaqabbalan.

O Allah, I ask You for beneficial knowledge, wholesome provision, and deeds that are accepted.

Phonetic transcription

Reference: Ibn As-Sunni, no. 54, Ibn Majah no. 925, Ibn Al-Qayyim 2/375

English

## 118 PRAYER FOR A GOOD REPUTATION AND A PROSPEROUS FUTURE

رَبِّ هَبۡ لِي حُكۡمٗا وَأَلۡحِقۡنِي بِٱلصَّٰلِحِينَ وَٱجۡعَل لِّي لِسَانَ صِدۡقٖ فِي ٱلۡأٓخِرِينَ وَٱجۡعَلۡنِي مِن وَرَثَةِ جَنَّةِ ٱلنَّعِيمِ.

Arabic

Rabbi hab li hukman wa alhiqni bissaliheen. Waj'al li lisanan sidiqan fil-akhireen. Waj'alni min waratati jannati an-naeem.

O Allah, grant me wisdom and join me with the righteous. Grant me an honorable mention among later generations. Make me one of the inheritors of the Garden of Bliss.

Phonetic transcription

Reference: Surat Ash-Shuara (26:83-85)

English

## 119 PRAYER TO INCREASE THE KNOWLEDGE

رَّبِّ زِدۡنِي عِلۡمٗا.

Arabic

Rabbi zidni ilma.

O Allah, increase my knowledge.

Phonetic transcription

Reference: Surat Ta-Ha (20:114)

English

## 120 PRAYER FOR HELP ACCEPTING FATE

رَبَّنَآ ءَاتِنَا مِن لَّدُنكَ رَحۡمَةٗ وَهَيِّئۡ لَنَا مِنۡ أَمۡرِنَا رَشَدٗا.

Arabic

Rabbana atina min ladunka rahmah wa hayyi' lana min amrina rashada.

O Allah, grant us mercy from Your presence and prepare for us guidance in our affairs.

Phonetic transcription

Reference: Surat Al-Kahf (18:10)

English

# 121 PRAYER FOR SUCCESS IN ALL AREAS

اللَّهُمَّ إِنِّي أَعُوذُ بِكَ مِنْ مُنْكَرَاتِ الْأَخْلَاقِ، وَالْأَعْمَالِ، وَالْأَهْوَاءِ.

Arabic

Allahumma inni a'udhu bika min munkarati lakhlaq, wa l'amal, wa l'ahwa'.

Phonetic transcription

Reference: Riyad as-Salihin 1482

O Allah, I seek refuge in You from immoral manners, actions, and desires.

English

# Prayers for well-being and contentment

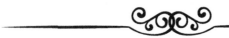

## 122 PRAYER FOR WELL-BEING AND PROTECTION FROM EVIL

اللَّهُمَّ إِنِّي أَسْأَلُكَ مِنَ الْخَيْرِ كُلِّهِ عَاجِلِهِ وَآجِلِهِ مَا عَلِمْتُ مِنْهُ وَمَا لَمْ أَعْلَمْ وَأَعُوذُ بِكَ مِنَ الشَّرِّ كُلِّهِ عَاجِلِهِ وَآجِلِهِ
مَا عَلِمْتُ مِنْهُ وَمَا لَمْ أَعْلَمْ اللَّهُمَّ إِنِّي أَسْأَلُكَ مِنْ خَيْرِ مَا سَأَلَكَ عَبْدُكَ وَنَبِيُّكَ وَأَعُوذُ بِكَ مِنْ شَرِّ مَا عَاذَ بِهِ عَبْدُكَ
وَنَبِيُّكَ اللَّهُمَّ إِنِّي أَسْأَلُكَ الْجَنَّةَ وَمَا قَرَّبَ إِلَيْهَا مِنْ قَوْلٍ أَوْ عَمَلٍ وَأَعُوذُ بِكَ مِنَ النَّارِ وَمَا قَرَّبَ إِلَيْهَا مِنْ قَوْلٍ أَوْ
عَمَلٍ وَأَسْأَلُكَ أَنْ تَجْعَلَ كُلَّ قَضَاءٍ قَضَيْتَهُ لِي خَيْرًا.

Arabic

Allahumma, inni as-aluka min alkhayri kullihi, aajilihi wa 'ajilihi, ma 'alimtu minhu wa ma lam a'lam. Wa a'udhu bika mina sharri kullihi, aajilihi wa 'ajilihi, ma 'alimtu minhu wa ma lam a'lam. Allahumma, inni as-alu-ka min khayri ma sa-alaka 'abduka wa nabiyyuka, wa a'udhu bika min sharri ma aadha bihi 'abduka wa nabiyyuka. Allahumma, inni as-alu-ka lJannata wa ma qarraba ilayha min qawlin aw 'amalin, wa a'udhu bika mina Nari wa ma qarraba ilayha min qawlin aw 'amalin. Wa as-aluka an taj'al kulla qada'in qadaytahu li khayran.

Reference: Sunan Ibn Majah 3846

O Allah, I ask You for all the good, whether immediate or delayed, that I know and that I am not aware of. I seek refuge in You from all evil, whether immediate or delayed, that I know and that I am not aware of. O Allah, I ask You for the good that Your servant and Your Prophet have asked You for, and I seek refuge in You from the evil that Your servant and Your Prophet sought refuge in. O Allah, I ask You for Paradise and whatever is close to it in speech or action, and I seek refuge in You from the Hellfire and whatever is close to it in speech or action. I ask You to make every decree You have decreed for me good.

Phonetic transcription

English

## 123 PRAYER FOR A GOOD LIFE IN THIS WORLD AND IN THE HEREAFTER

اللَّهُمَّ أَصْلِحْ لِي دِينِيَ الَّذِي هُوَ عِصْمَةُ أَمْرِي وَأَصْلِحْ لِي دُنْيَايَ الَّتِي فِيهَا مَعَاشِي وَأَصْلِحْ لِي آخِرَتِي
الَّتِي فِيهَا مَعَادِي وَاجْعَلِ الْحَيَاةَ زِيَادَةً لِي فِي كُلِّ خَيْرٍ وَاجْعَلِ الْمَوْتَ رَاحَةً لِي مِنْ كُلِّ شَرٍّ.

Arabic

Allahumma, aslih li deeni alladi huwa 'ismatu amri, wa aslih li dunyaya allati feeha ma'ashi, wa aslih li akhirati allati feeha ma'adi. Waj'ali l-hayata ziyadatan li fi kulli khayr, wa waj'ali l-mawta raḥatan li min kulli shar.

Reference: Riyad as-Salihin 1472

O Allah, rectify my religion, which is the safeguard of my affairs, and rectify my worldly life, in which is my livelihood, and rectify my Hereafter, to which is my return. Make life an increase for me in every goodness, and make death a comfort for me from every evil.

Phonetic transcription

English

## 124 PRAYER FOR FORGIVENESS AND PROSPERITY

اللَّهُمَّ اغْفِرْ لِي ذَنْبِي وَوَسِّ لِي فِي دَارِي وَبَارِكْ لِي فِيمَا رَزَقْتَنِي.

Arabic

Allahumma, ghfir li dhambi wa wassi` li fi daari wa barik li fi ma razaqtani.

Reference: Jami' at-Tirmidhi 3500

O Allah, forgive my sins, expand my abode, and bless what You have provided for me.

Phonetic transcription

English

## 125 PRAYER FOR BLESSING THE HOMELAND

اللَّهُمَّ ضَعْ فِي أَرْضِنَا بَرَكَتَهَا، وَزِينَتَهُ، وَسَكَنَهَا.

Arabic

Allahumma da' fi ardina barakataha wa zinataha wa sakanaha.

O Allah! Put blessings, beauty and calm in our land.

Reference: Al-Mu'jam al-Kabir (Al-Tabarani)

Phonetic transcription

English

## 126 PRAYER FOR HAVING OFFSPRING

رَبِّ هَبْ لِي مِن لَّدُنكَ ذُرِّيَّةً طَيِّبَةً إِنَّكَ سَمِيعُ ٱلدُّعَآءِ.

Arabic

Rabbi hab li min ladunka dhuriyatan tayyibatan. Innaka Sami'u d-dua.

O Allah, grant me from Your presence a good offspring. Indeed, You are the Hearer of supplication.

Reference: Surat Al Imran (3:38)

Phonetic transcription

English

## 127 PRAYER FOR A SUFFICIENT SUPPLY OF FOOD

ٱللَّهُمَّ أَنزِلْ عَلَيْنَا مَآئِدَةً مِّنَ ٱلسَّمَآءِ تَكُونُ لَنَا عِيدًا لِّأَوَّلِنَا وَءَاخِرِنَا وَءَايَةً مِّنكَ وَٱرْزُقْنَا وَأَنتَ خَيْرُ ٱلرَّٰزِقِينَ.

Arabic

Allahumma, Rabbana anzil 'alayna ma'idatan mina s-sama' takunu lana 'idan li-awalina wa akhirina wa ayatam minka. Warzuqna wa anta khayru razqeen.

O Allah, our Lord, send down to us a table spread from the heavens to be a festival for us, for the first of us and the last of us, and a sign from You. And provide for us; You are the best of providers.

Reference: Surat Al-Maidah (5:114)

Phonetic transcription

English

# 128 PRAYER FOR HAPPINESS AND PROSPERITY

اللهم قَنِعنِـي بِمـا رزقتَنِي وبارِك لِي فِيه واخْلُف علي كُل غَائِبَةٍ بِخيرٍ.

Arabic

Allahumma, qannini bima razaqtani wa barik li fihi wa khluf 'alayya kulla ghaa'ibatin bikhayr.

O Allah, content me with what You have provided for me, bless it for me, and replace any loss with something better.

Reference: Al-Adab Al-Mufrad 681

Phonetic transcription

English

# 129 PRAYER TO MORALIZE THE LOOK IN THE MIRROR

اللَّهُمَّ أَنْتَ حَسَّنْتَ خَلْقِي فَحَسِّنْ خُلُقِي.

Arabic

Allahuma 'anta hasanta khalqi fahasin khuluqi.

O Allah You have made my creation perfect, so make my moral characteristics also be the best.

Reference: Bulugh al-Maram

Phonetic transcription

English

# 130 PRAYER FOR HELP AGAINST SADNESS AND SORROW

اللهمَّ إني عبدُك ابنُ عبدِك ابنُ أمَتِك، ناصيَتي بيدِك، ماضٍ فيَّ حُكمُك، عَدْلٌ فيَّ قضاؤُك، أسألُك بكلِّ اسمٍ هو لك سميت به نفسَك أوْ علَّمْتَهُ أحدًا مِنْ خلقِك أو أنزلته في كتابِك أو استأثرتَ به في علمِ الغيبِ عندَك أنْ تجعلَ القرآنَ ربيعَ قلبي ونورَ صدري وجلاءَ حُزني وذهابَ هَمّي.

Arabic

Allahumma, inni 'abduka ibnu 'abdika ibnu amatik. Nasīyati biyadik, madin fiyya hukmuk, 'adlun fiyya qada'uk. As'aluka bismika l-ladhi samayta bihi nafsak, aw allamtahu ahadan min khalqik, aw anzaltahu fi kitabik, aw asta'tarta bihi fi 'ilmi lghayb 'indak, an taj'ala l-Qur'ana rabī'a qalbi wa nura sadri, wa jlā'a huzani, wa dhahab hammī.

O Allah, I am Your servant, the son of Your servant, the son of Your maidservant. You have absolute control over me and Your decision concerning me prevails. Your justice is my defense, and Your decree upon me is just. I ask You by every name You have named Yourself, taught to any of Your creation, or revealed in Your Book, or kept in the unseen with You, to make the Qur'an the delight of my heart, the light of my chest, the dispeller of my sadness, and the reliever of my distress.

Reference: Ahmad 1/391

Phonetic transcription

English

# 131 PRAYER FOR ALLAH'S ASSISTANCE

رَبَّنَا وَاجْعَلْنَا مُسْلِمَيْنِ لَكَ وَمِن ذُرِّيَّتِنَا أُمَّةً مُّسْلِمَةً لَّكَ وَأَرِنَا مَنَاسِكَنَا وَتُبْ عَلَيْنَا ۖ إِنَّكَ أَنتَ التَّوَّابُ الرَّحِيمُ .

Rabbana taqabbal minna, innaka Anta Sami'u l'Alim. Rabbana waj'alna muslimayni laka, wa min dhurriyatina ummatan muslimatan laka, wa arina manasikana, wa tub 'alayna. Innaka Anta Tawabu Rahim.


Arabic

Reference: Surat Al-Baqarah

Our Lord, accept from us. Indeed, You are the Hearing, the Knowing. Our Lord, make both of us submissive to You, and raise from our descendants a community submissive to You. And show us our ways of worship, and turn towards us. Surely, You are the Most-Relenting, Most-Merciful.

# 132 PRAYER FOR THE RIGHT GUIDANCE ON THE WAY TO ISLAM

ربَّنَا أَصْلِح بَيْنَنَا وَاهْدِنَا سَبِيلَ الإِسلام وَنَجِّنَا مِن الظُّلمَات إِلَى النُّور ، واصرِف عَنَّا الفَوَاحِشَ مَا ظَهَر مِنها ومَا بَطَن وبَارِك لَنا في أسماعِنا وأبصارِنا وقُلوبِنا وأزواجِنا وذُرِّياتِنا ، وتُب علينا إِنَّكَ أنت التَّوَّابُ الرَّحِيم ، واجعَلنا شاكِرين لِنِعمَتِك مُثنِين بِها قائِلين بِها وأتمِمهَا علينا .

Rabbana aslih baynana wahdina sabila al-Islam wanjina min adh-dhulamati ila an-nur. Wasrif 'anna al-fawahisha ma thahara minha wa ma batan. Barik lana fi asma'ina wa absarina wa qulubina wa azwajina wa dhurriyatina. Watauba 'alayna innaka Anta at-Tawwabu ar-Rahim. Waj'alna shakireen li-ni'matika muthnina biha qailin biha wa atmimha 'alayna.


Arabic

Reference: Al-Adab Al-Mufrad 630

Our Lord, make peace between us and guide us on the path of Islam. Save us from the darkness into the light. Remove acts of deviance from us, both open and hidden. Bless our hearing, our sight, our hearts, our wives and our children. Turn towards us; indeed, You are the Most-Relenting, Most-Merciful. And make us grateful for Your favors, acknowledging it, praising it, and completing it for us.

# 133 PRAYER FOR STRONG FAITH AND SUPPORT

اللَّهُمَّ اقْسِمْ لَنَا مِنْ خَشْيَتِكَ مَا يَحُولُ بَيْنَنَا وَبَيْنَ مَعَاصِيكَ وَمِنْ طَاعَتِكَ مَا تُبَلِّغُنَا بِهِ جَنَّتَكَ وَمِنْ الْيَقِينِ مَا تُهَوِّنُ بِهِ عَلَيْنَا مُصِيبَاتِ الدُّنْيَا وَمَتِّعْنَا بِأَسْمَاعِنَا وَأَبْصَارِنَا وَقُوَّتِنَا مَا أَحْيَيْتَنَا وَاجْعَلْهُ الْوَارِثَ مِنَّا وَاجْعَلْ ثَأْرَنَا عَلَى مَنْ ظَلَمَنَا وَانْصُرْنَا عَلَى مَنْ عَادَانَا وَلَا تَجْعَلْ مُصِيبَتَنَا فِي دِينِنَا وَلَا تَجْعَلِ الدُّنْيَا أَكْبَرَ هَمِّنَا وَلَا مَبْلَغَ عِلْمِنَا وَلَا تُسَلِّطْ عَلَيْنَا مَنْ لَا يَرْحَمُنَا .

Allahumma, qsim lana min khashyatika ma yahulu baynana wa bayna ma'asiyik wa min ta'atika ma tuballighuna bihi Jannatak, wa mina l-yaqini ma tuhawwinu bihi 'alayna musibati d-dunya. wa mati'na bi-asma'ina wa absarina wa quwwatina ma ahyaitana, waj'alhu l-waritha minna, waj'al tharana 'ala man dalamana, wa nsurna 'ala man 'adana, wa la taj'al musibatana fi dinina, wa la taj'ali d-dunya akbara hammina, wa la mablagha 'ilmina, wa la tusalit 'alayna man la yarhamuna.


Arabic

Reference: Jami' at-Tirmidhi 3502

O Allah, grant for us such awe of You that will serve as a barrier between Your disobedience and us. Grant us such obedience by which we may attain Your Paradise. Bestow upon us the certainty that will lighten the calamities of this world for us. Bless us with the use of our hearing, sight, and strength as long as You grant us life. Make our revenge be upon those who wrong us, and help us against our enemies. Do not let our affliction be in our religion, and do not make the world our greatest concern, nor the extent of our knowledge, and do not give authority over us to those who will not show us mercy.

## 134 PRAYER FOR GOOD DURING A STORM

اللَّهُمَّ إِنِّي أَسْأَلُكَ مِنْ خَيْرِ مَا أُرْسِلَتْ بِهِ، وَأَعُوذُ بِكَ مِنْ شَرِّ مَا أُرْسِلَتْ بِهِ.

Arabic

Allahumma, inni as'aluka min khayri ma ursila bihi, wa a'udhu bika min sharri ma ursila bihi.

O Allah, I ask You for the good of what it has been sent with, and I seek refuge in You from the evil of what it has been sent with.

Phonetic transcription

Reference: Muslim 2/616, Al-Bukhari 4/76

English

## 135 PRAYER AGAINST CALAMITY

اللَّهُمَّ حَوَالَيْنَا وَلَا عَلَيْنَا اللَّهُمَّ عَلَى الْآكَامِ وَالْجِبَالِ وَالْآجَامِ وَالظِّرَابِ وَالْأَوْدِيَةِ وَمَنَابِتِ الشَّجَرِ.

Arabic

Allahumma hawalayna wa la 'alayna, Allahumma 'ala l-akami wal-jibali wal-ajami wal-dhirabi wal-awdiyati wa manabiti shajar.

O Allah, let the rain fall around us and not upon us, O Allah, let it fall on the pastures, hills, valleys, and the roots of trees.

Phonetic transcription

Reference: Al-Bukhari 1/224, Muslim 1/614

English

## 136 PRAYER FOR SAFETY DURING A THUNDERSTORM

اللَّهُمَّ لَا تَقْتُلْنَا بِغَضَبِكَ وَلَا تُهْلِكْنَا بِعَذَابِكَ وَعَافِنَا قَبْلَ ذَٰلِكَ.

Arabic

Allahumma la taqtulna bighadabika wa la tuhlikna bi'adhabika wa 'afina qabla dhalik.

O Allah, do not kill us in Your anger, nor destroy us with Your punishment, and grant us well-being before that.

Phonetic transcription

Reference: Jami' at-Tirmidhi 3450

English

## 137 PRAYER FOR COURAGE AND BALANCE

اللهمَّ إنِّي أعُوذُ بِكَ مِنْ جَهْدِ الْبَلَاءِ، وَدَرَكِ الشَّقَاءِ، وَسُوءِ الْقَضَاءِ، وَشَمَاتَةِ الْأَعْدَاءِ.

Arabic

Allahumma inni a'udhu bika min jahdil bala', wa darki shaqa', wa soo'il qada', wa shamatati l-a'da'.

Phonetic transcription

O Allah, I seek Your protection from severe calamity, widespread misery, unfavorable circumstances, and the mockery of enemies.

English

Reference:
(Bukhari and Muslim.)
Al-Adab Al-Mufrad 729

## 138 PRAYER FOR SATISFACTION AND GRATITUDE

اللّهُـمَّ ما أَصْبَـحَ بي مِـنْ نِعْـمَةٍ أَو بِأَحَـدٍ مِـنْ خَلْـقِك، فَمِـنْكَ وَحْـدَكَ لا شريكَ لَـك، فَلَـكَ الْحَمْـدُ وَلَـكَ الشُّكْـرُ.

Arabic

Allahumma ma asbaha bi min ni'matin aw bi ahadin min khalqika, faminka wahdaka la sharika lak, falaka l-hamdu walaka sh-shukr.

Phonetic transcription

O Allah, whatever blessing has been received by me or anyone of Your creation 1 is from You alone, You have no partner. All praise is for You and thanks are for You.

English

Reference: Abu Dawud 4/318

## 139 PRAYER FOR WELL-BEING

رَضِيتُ بِاللَّهِ رَبًّا وَبِالْإِسْلَامِ دِينًا وَبِمُحَمَّدٍ نَبِيًّا.

Arabic

Raḍītu billāhi rabban wa bil Islāmi dīnan wa bi muḥammadin nabiyyan.

Phonetic transcription

I am pleased with Allah as my Lord, with Islam as my religion, and with Muhammad as my Prophet.

English

Reference:
At-Tirmidhi 5/465

## 140 PRAYER FOR BLESSING THE BELOVED ONES

رَبَّنَا ٱغۡفِرۡ لِي وَلِوَٰلِدَيَّ وَلِلۡمُؤۡمِنِينَ يَوۡمَ يَقُومُ ٱلۡحِسَابُ.

Arabic

Rabbanaa ighfir lii wa li waalidayya wa li'l-mu'miniina yawma yaqoomu al-hisaab.

Phonetic transcription

O Allah, forgive me, my parents and all the believers on the Day of Judgment.

English

Reference: Surat Ibrahim (14:41)

## 141 PRAYER FOR A RIGHTEOUS OFFSPRING

رَبِّ هَبۡ لِي مِنَ ٱلصَّٰلِحِينَ.

Arabic

Rabbi hablii mina as-saaliheen.

Phonetic transcription

O Allah, give me a righteous child.

English

Reference: Surat As-Saaffat (37:100)

## 142 PRAYER FOR ACCESSING PARADISE

رَبِّ ٱبۡنِ لِي عِندَكَ بَيۡتٗا فِي ٱلۡجَنَّةِ.

Arabic

Rabbi ibni lee 'indaka baytan fil-Jannah.

Phonetic transcription

O Allah, build a house for me near You in Paradise.

English

Reference: Surat At-Tahreem (66:11)

# 143 PRAYER FOR BLESSING THE FAMILY AND MARRIAGE

رَبَّنَا هَبْ لَنَا مِنْ أَزْوَٰجِنَا وَذُرِّيَّٰتِنَا قُرَّةَ أَعْيُنٍ وَٱجْعَلْنَا لِلْمُتَّقِينَ إِمَامًا.

Arabic

Rabbana hab lana min azwajina wa dhuriyatina qurrata 'aayunin waj'alna lilmuttaqina imama.

O Allah, grant us from our spouses and offspring comfort to our eyes, and make us an example for the righteous.

Phonetic transcription

Reference: Surat Al-Furqan (25:74)

English

# 144 PRAYER FOR LOVE

اللَّهُمَّ إِنِّي أَسأَلُكَ فِعْلَ الْخَيْرَاتِ، وَتَرْكَ الْمُنْكَرَاتِ، وَحُبَّ الْمَسَاكِينِ، وَأَنْ تَغْفِرَ لِي، وَتَرْحَمَنِي، وَإِذَا أَرَدْتَ فِتْنَةَ قَوْمٍ فَتَوَفَّنِي غَيْرَ مَفْتُونٍ، وَأَسْأَلُكَ حُبَّكَ، وَحُبَّ مَنْ يُحِبُّكَ، وَحُبَّ عَمَلٍ يُقَرِّبُنِي إِلَى حُبِّكَ.

Arabic

Allahumma inni as'aluka fe'ila l-khayrat, wa tarka l-munkarat, wa hubba l-masakin, wa an taghfira li wa tarhamani. Wa idha aradta fitnata qawmin, fatawaffani ghayra maf-tunin. Wa as'aluka hubbaka, wa hubba man yuhibbuka, wa hubba amalin yuqarribuni ila hubbika.

O Allah, I ask You for the performance of good deeds, avoiding evil deeds, love for the poor, and that You forgive me and have mercy for me. When You intend to test a people, grant me death without being tested. I ask for Your love, the love of those who love You, and the love of deeds that will bring me closer to Your love.

Reference: Jami' at-Tirmidhi 3235

Phonetic transcription

English

# 145 PRAYER FOR GUIDANCE AND PIETY

اللَّهُمَّ إِنِّي أَسْأَلُكَ الهُدَى، وَالتُّقَى، وَالعفَافَ، والغنَى.

Arabic

Allahumma inni as'aluka l-huda wa tuqa wa l-'afafa wa l-ghina.

O Allah! I ask You for guidance, piety, chastity and self- sufficiency.

Phonetic transcription

Reference: Riyad as-Salihin 71

English

# Prayers for self-improvement

## 146 PRAYER FOR TURNING AWAY FROM WEAKNESSES OF CHARACTER

اللَّهُمَّ إِنِّي أَعُوذُ بِكَ مِنْ مُنْكَرَاتِ الأَخْلَاقِ، وَالأَعْمَالِ، وَالأَهْوَاءِ.

Arabic

Allahuma 'iniy 'aeudh bika min munkarati l'akhlaqi, wa l'aemali, wa l'ahwa'.

O Allah, I seek refuge in You from immoral conduct, deeds, and desires.

Phonetic transcription

Reference: Mishkat al-Masabih 2471

English

## 147 PRAYER FOR A GOOD CHARACTER

رَبَّنَا أَتْمِمْ لَنَا نُورَنَا وَاغْفِرْ لَنَا إِنَّكَ عَلَى كُلِّ شَيْءٍ قَدِيرٌ.

Arabic

Rabbana atmim lana noorana wa ghfir lana. Innaka 'ala kulli shay'in qadeer.

O Allah, perfect our light and forgive us. Indeed, You are capable of all things.

Phonetic transcription

Reference: Surat At-Tahreem (66:8)

English

## 148 PRAYER FOR CHARACTER AND STEADFASTNESS

اللَّهُمَّ إِنِّي أَسْأَلُكَ الثَّبَاتَ فِي الأَمْرِ، وَالْعَزِيمَةَ عَلَى الرُّشْدِ، وَأَسْأَلُكَ مُوجِبَاتِ رَحْمَتِكَ، وَعَزَائِمَ مَغْفِرَتِكَ، وَأَسْأَلُكَ شُكْرَ نِعْمَتِكَ، وَحُسْنَ عِبَادَتِكَ، وَأَسْأَلُكَ قَلْباً سَلِيماً، وَلِسَاناً صَادِقاً، وَأَسْأَلُكَ مِنْ خَيْرِ مَا تَعْلَمُ، وَأَعُوذُ بِكَ مِنْ شَرِّ مَا تَعْلَمُ، وَأَسْتَغْفِرُكَ لِمَا تَعْلَمُ.

Arabic

Allahumma inni as-aluka athabata fi l-amri, wa l-'azimata 'ala rrushdi. Wa as-aluka mujibati rahmatika, wa 'aza'ima maghfiratika. Wa as-aluka shukra ni'matika, wa husna 'ibadatika. Wa as-aluka qalban saliman, wa lisanan sadiqan. Wa as-aluka min khayri ma ta'lamu, wa a'udhu bika min sharri ma ta'lamu. Wa astaghfiruka lima ta'lamu.

O Allah, make me strong in doing good, help me stay on the right path, and shower me with Your mercy and forgiveness. Grant me gratitude for Your blessings, the ability to worship You sincerely, and a pure heart and truthful tongue. I ask for the best things in life, and seek refuge from anything harmful. Please forgive me for what You know about me.

Phonetic transcription

Reference: Sunan an-Nasa'i 1304

English

## 149 PRAYER FOR STRENGTH IN FAITH

اللَّهُمَّ إِنِّي عَبْدُكَ، ابْنُ عَبْدِكَ، ابْنُ أَمَتِكَ، نَاصِيَتِي بِيَدِكَ، مَاضٍ فِيَّ حُكْمُكَ، عَدْلٌ فِيَّ قَضَاؤُكَ، أَسْأَلُكَ بِكُلِّ اسْمٍ هُوَ لَكَ سَمَّيْتَ بِهِ نَفْسَكَ، أَوْ أَنْزَلْتَهُ فِي كِتَابِكَ، أَوْ عَلَّمْتَهُ أَحَدًا مِنْ خَلْقِكَ، أَوِ اسْتَأْثَرْتَ بِهِ فِي عِلْمِ الْغَيْبِ عِنْدَكَ، أَنْ تَجْعَلَ الْقُرْآنَ رَبِيعَ قَلْبِي، وَنُورَ صَدْرِي، وَجَلَاءَ وَذَهَابَ هَمِّي.

Arabic

Allahumma inni 'abduka, ibnu 'abdika, ibnu amatika. Nasīyati biyadika, māḍin fiyya ḥukmuka, 'adlun fiyya qaḍā'uka. As'aluka bī kulli smin huwa laka sammayta bihi nafsak, aw anzaltahu fī kitābika, aw 'allamtahu aḥadan min khalqika, aw ista'tharta bihi fī 'ilmi l-ghaybi 'indak, an taj'ala l-Qur'āna rabī'a qalbī, wa nūra ṣadrī, wa jalā'a ḥuznī, wa dhahāba hamī.

Reference: Ahmad 1/391

O Allah, I am Your servant, the son of Your servant, the son of Your maidservant. My forehead is in Your hand; Your command over me is forever executed, and Your decree over me is just. I ask You by every name belonging to You which You have named Yourself with, revealed in Your Book, taught anyone from Your creation, or kept unto Yourself in the unseen knowledge, to make the Quran the joy of my heart, the light of my heart, the banisher of my sadness, and the reliever of my distress.

Phonetic transcription | English

## 150 PRAYER FOR THE SUPPORT OF FAITH

اللَّهُمَّ مُصَرِّفَ الْقُلُوبِ صَرِّفْ قُلُوبَنَا عَلَى طَاعَتِكَ.

Arabic

Qul allahumma a'nī 'alā dhikrika wa shukrika wa husni 'ibādatik.

Reference: Abu Dawud 2/86, An-Nasa'i 3/53

Say: O Allah, help me in remembering You, expressing gratitude to You, and worshiping You in the best manner.

Phonetic transcription | English

## 151 PRAYER FOR OBEDIENCE AND STRONG FAITH

اللَّهُمَّ حَبِّبْ إِلَينَا الإيمَانَ، وَزَيِّنْهُ فِي قُلُوبِنَا، وَكَرِّهْ إِلَينَا الكُفْرَ وَالفُسُوقَ وَالعِصْيَانَ، وَاجْعَنَا مِن الرَّاشِدِينَ، اللَّهُمَّ أَحْيِنَا مُسْلِمِينَ وتَوَفَّنَا مُسْلِمِينَ، وَأَلْحِقْنَا بِالصَّالحينَ، غيرَ خَزَايَا وَلا مَفْتُونِينَ .

Arabic

Allahumma habbib ilayna al-imana wa zayinhu fi qulubina, wa karrih ilayna al-kufra wa l-fusuqa wa l-'isyana, waj'alna mina r-rashidin. Allahumma tawaffana muslimina wa ah-yina muslimina wa alhiqna bissaliheen ghayra khazaya wala mftunin.

Reference: Al-Adab Al-Mufrad 699

O Allah, make faith beloved to us and beautify it in our hearts. Make disbelief, wickedness, and disobedience hateful to us, and grant us guidance to be among the righteous. O Allah, let us die as Muslims and live as Muslims, and join us with the righteous without disgrace or temptation.

Phonetic transcription | English

## 152 PRAYER FOR A PURE SOUL & FEAR OF GOD

اللَّهُمَّ آتِ نَفْسِي تَقْوَاهَا وَزَكِّهَا أَنْتَ خَيْرُ مَنْ زَكَّاهَا أَنْتَ وَلِيُّهَا وَمَوْلاَهَا اللَّهُمَّ إِنِّي أَعُوذُ بِكَ مِنْ عِلْمٍ لاَ يَنْفَعُ وَمِنْ قَلْبٍ لاَ يَخْشَعُ وَمِنْ نَفْسٍ لاَ تَشْبَعُ وَمِنْ دَعْوَةٍ لاَ يُسْتَجَابُ لَهَا .

Arabic

O Allah, ātī nafsī taqwāhā, wa zakkīhā Anta khayru man zakkāhā, Anta waliyyuhā wa mawlāhā, Allahumma innī a'ūdhu bika min 'ilmin lā yanfa', wa min qalbin lā yakhsha', wa min nafsin lā tashba', wa min du'atin lā yustajābu laha.

Phonetic transcription

Reference: Sahih Muslim 2722, Sunan an-Nasā'ī 5458

O Allah, grant my soul its piety, and purify it for You are the best to purify it. You are its Guardian and Master. O Allah, I seek refuge in You from knowledge that is of no benefit, from a heart that does not humble, from a soul that is never satisfied, and from a supplication that is not answered.

English

## 153 PRAYER FOR GUIDANCE TO THE RIGHT PATH

اللَّهُمَّ اهْدِنِي وَسَدِّدْنِي وَاذْكُرْ بِالْهُدَى هِدَايَتَكَ الطَّرِيقَ.

Arabic

Allahuma ahdini wasadidni wadhkur bialhudaa hidayataka tariqa.

Phonetic transcription

Reference: Sahih Muslim 2725a

O Allah, guide me, make me steadfast, and remember with guidance the path You lead.

English

## 154 PRAYER FOR A DUE SUBMISSION

عَلَى ٱللَّهِ تَوَكَّلْنَا رَبَّنَا لَا تَجْعَلْنَا فِتْنَةً لِّلْقَوْمِ ٱلظَّٰلِمِينَ، وَنَجِّنَا بِرَحْمَتِكَ مِنَ ٱلْقَوْمِ ٱلْكَٰفِرِينَ.

Arabic

Alā 'llāhi tawakkalnā, rabbanā lā taj'alnā fitnatan lil-qawmi dālimīn, wa najjinā bi raḥmatika mina l-qawmi l-kāfirīn.

Phonetic transcription

Reference: Surat Yunus (10:85-86)

In Allah, we place our trust. O Allah, do not make us a trial for the wrongdoing people; and save us, by Your mercy, from the disbelieving people.

English

## 155 PRAYER FOR AN INCREASE IN SPIRITUALITY

اللَّهمَّ أعنِّي على ذِكْرِك، وشُكْرِك، وحُسنِ عبادتِك.

Arabic

Allahumma a'nī 'alā dhikrika wa shukrika wa husni 'ibādatik.

O Allah, help me in remembering You, expressing gratitude to You, and worshiping You in the best manner.

Phonetic transcription

Reference
Abu Dawud 2/86,
An-Nasa'i 3/53

English

## 156 PRAYER FOR AVOIDING THE SINS

اللَّهمَّ إنِّي أعوذُ بِكَ مِن منكَراتِ الأخلاقِ، والأعمَالِ والأهْواءِ.

Arabic

Allahumma inni a'udhu bika min munkarati l'akhlaqi, wal-a'mali, wal-ahwa'i.

O Allah, I seek refuge in You from the evils of manners, actions, and desires.

Phonetic transcription

Reference: Riyad as-Salihin 1482

English

## 157 PRAYER FOR RIGHTEOUSNESS AND GRATITUDE

رَبِّ أَوْزِعْنِيٓ أَنْ أَشْكُرَ نِعْمَتَكَ ٱلَّتِيٓ أَنْعَمْتَ عَلَيَّ وَعَلَىٰ وَٰلِدَيَّ وَأَنْ أَعْمَلَ صَٰلِحًا تَرْضَىٰهُ وَأَدْخِلْنِي
بِرَحْمَتِكَ فِي عِبَادِكَ ٱلصَّٰلِحِينَ.

Arabic

Rabbi awwiz'ni an ashkura ni'mataka lati an'amta 'alayya wa 'ala walidayya wa an a'mala salihan tardahu wa adkhilni biraḥmatika fi 'ibadika ṣāliḥīn.

O Allah, enable me to be grateful for Your favor which You have bestowed upon me and upon my parents, and to work righteousness of which You approve, and admit me, by Your mercy, among Your righteous servants.

Phonetic transcription

Reference: Surat An-Naml (27:19)

English

# 158 PRAYER FOR MORE PATIENCE AND A DEATH AS A MUSLIM

رَبَّنَآ أَفۡرِغۡ عَلَيۡنَا صَبۡرٗا وَتَوَفَّنَا مُسۡلِمِينَ.

Arabic

Rabbana frigh 'alayna sabran wa tawaffana muslimin.

O Allah, pour upon us patience and let us die as Muslims.

Phonetic transcription

Reference: Surat Al-Araf (7:126)

English

# 159 PRAYER FOR MORE SELF-CONFIDENCE

رَبِّ ٱشۡرَحۡ لِي صَدۡرِي وَيَسِّرۡ لِيٓ أَمۡرِي وَٱحۡلُلۡ عُقۡدَةٗ مِّن لِّسَانِي يَفۡقَهُواْ قَوۡلِي.

Arabic

Rabbi ishrah li sadri wa yassir li amri, waahlul 'uqdatan min lisaani yafqahu qawli.

O Allah, open up my heart, ease my task for me, and remove the impediment from my speech so that they may understand my words.

Phonetic transcription

Reference: Surat Taha (20:25-28)

English

# 160 PRAYER FOR A STRONG ATTACHMENT TO FAITH AND SPIRITUALITY

يَا مُقَلِّبَ الْقُلُوبِ ثَبِّتْ قَلْبِي عَلَى دِينِكَ.

Arabic

Yā muqalliba lqulūbi thabbit qalbī `alā dīnik.

O changer of the hearts, make my heart firm upon Your religion.

Phonetic transcription

Reference: Jami' at-Tirmidhi 3587

English

# 161 PRAYER FOR A STRONG FAITH IN THE FAMILY

رَبِّ ٱجْعَلْنِي مُقِيمَ ٱلصَّلَوٰةِ وَمِن ذُرِّيَّتِيۚ رَبَّنَا وَتَقَبَّلْ دُعَآءِ.

Arabic

Rabbi ij'alni muqema salati wa min dhuriyati. Rabbana wataqabbal du'a.

O Allah, make me one who establishes prayer, and also, my descendants. O Allah, accept my supplication.

Phonetic transcription

Reference: Surat Ibrahim (14:40)

English

# 162 PRAYER FOR A PURE SOUL

رَبَّنَا ظَلَمْنَآ أَنفُسَنَا وَإِن لَّمْ تَغْفِرْ لَنَا وَتَرْحَمْنَا لَنَكُونَنَّ مِنَ ٱلْخَٰسِرِينَ.

Arabic

Rabbana dhalamna anfusana wa'in lam taghfir lana wa tarhamna lanakoonanna mina alkhasireen.

O Allah, we have wronged ourselves, and if You do not forgive us and have mercy upon us, we will surely be among the losers.

Phonetic transcription

Reference: Surat Al-Araf (7:23)

English

# 163 PRAYER FOR HELP AND SUPPORT

رَبَّنَآ ءَاتِنَا مِن لَّدُنكَ رَحْمَةً وَهَيِّئْ لَنَا مِنْ أَمْرِنَا رَشَدًا.

Arabic

Rabbana atina min ladunka rahmah wa hayyi' lana min amrina rashada.

O Allah, grant us mercy from Your presence and prepare for us guidance in our affairs.

Phonetic transcription

Reference: Surat Al-Kahf (18:10)

English

## 164 PRAYER FOR RIGHTEOUSNESS

رَبِّ أَوْزِعْنِيٓ أَنْ أَشْكُرَ نِعْمَتَكَ ٱلَّتِيٓ أَنْعَمْتَ عَلَيَّ وَعَلَىٰ وَٰلِدَيَّ وَأَنْ أَعْمَلَ صَٰلِحًا تَرْضَىٰهُ وَأَدْخِلْنِي
بِرَحْمَتِكَ فِي عِبَادِكَ ٱلصَّٰلِحِينَ.

Arabic

Rabbi awwiz'ni an ashkura ni'mataka lati an'amta 'alayya wa 'ala walidayya wa an a'mala salihan tardahu wa adkhilni birahmatika fi 'ibadika ṣāliḥīn.

Phonetic transcription

O Allah, enable me to be grateful for Your favor which You have bestowed upon me and upon my parents, and to work righteousness of which You approve, and admit me, by Your mercy, among Your righteous servants.

English

Reference: Surat An-Naml (27:19)

## 165 PRAYER FOR CONTROL (WHEN ANGRY)

أَعُوذُ بِاللَّهِ مِنَ الشَّيْطَانِ الرَّجِيمِ.

Arabic

A'ūdhu billāhi mina Shayṭāni rajīm.

Phonetic transcription

I seek refuge in Allah from Satan the outcast.

English

Reference: Al-Bukhari 7/99, Muslim 4/2015

## 166 PRAYER FOR PATIENCE

رَبَّنَآ أَفْرِغْ عَلَيْنَا صَبْرًا وَثَبِّتْ أَقْدَامَنَا وَٱنصُرْنَا عَلَى ٱلْقَوْمِ ٱلْكَٰفِرِينَ.

Arabic

Rabbana afrigh 'alayna sabra, wa thabbit aqdamana, wansurna 'ala al-qawmi l-kafireen.

Phonetic transcription

O Allah, pour upon us patience and plant firmly our feet and give us victory over the disbelieving people.

English

Reference: Surat Al-Baqarah (2:250)

# 167 PRAYER FOR HELP WITH UNCERTAINTY AND FEAR

بِسْمِ اللَّهِ الَّذِي لَا يَضُرُّ مَعَ اسْمِهِ شَيْءٌ فِي الْأَرْضِ وَلَا فِي السَّمَاءِ وَهُوَ السَّمِيعُ الْعَلِيمُ.

Arabic

Bismillāhi 'l-ladhī lā yaḍurru ma`a smihi shay'un fi l-'arḍi wa lā fi samā' wa huwa Samī `u l-`Alīm.

In the Name of Allah, by Whose Name nothing can cause harm in the earth nor in the heavens, except by His permission, and He is the All-Hearing, the All-Knowing.

Phonetic transcription

Reference: Abu Dawud 4/323, At-Tirmidhi 5/465, Ibn Majah 2/332, Ahmad

English

# 168 PRAYER FOR FRUGALITY

اللَّهُمَّ إِنِّي أَعُوذُ بِكَ مِنْ عِلْمٍ لاَ يَنْفَعُ وَمِنْ دُعَاءٍ لاَ يُسْمَعُ وَمَنْ قَلْبٍ لاَ يَخْشَعُ وَمِنْ نَفْسٍ لاَ تَشْبَعُ.

Arabic

Allahumma, inni a'udhu bika min 'ilmin la yanfa', wa mindu'a'in la yusma', wa min qalbin la yakhsha', wa min nafsin la tashba'.

O Allah, I seek refuge in You from knowledge that is of no benefit, from supplication that is not heard, from a heart that does not humble itself, and from a soul that is never satisfied.

Phonetic transcription

Reference: Sunan Ibn Majah 250

English

# 169 PRAYER AGAINST BELIEVING IN FALSE PROPHECIES

اللهُمَّ لاَ طَيْرَ إلا طَيْرُكَ وَلاَ خَيْرَ إِلَّا خَيْرُكَ وَلاَ إِلَهَ غَيْرُكَ.

Arabic

Allāhumma lā ṭayra illā ṭayruk, wa lā khayra illā khayruk, wa lā ilāha ghayruk.

O Allah, there is no prediction except those under Your control, and there is no goodness except the goodness You provide. There is no deity worthy of worship except You.

Phonetic transcription

Reference: Ahmad 2/220, Ibn As-Sunni (no. 292)

English

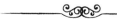

# Prayers for the welfare of others

## 170 PRAYER FOR BENEVOLENCE AND UNITY AMONG ALL BELIEVERS

رَبَّنَا ٱغْفِرْ لَنَا وَلِإِخْوَٰنِنَا ٱلَّذِينَ سَبَقُونَا بِٱلْإِيمَٰنِ وَلَا تَجْعَلْ فِي قُلُوبِنَا غِلًّا لِّلَّذِينَ ءَامَنُوا۟ رَبَّنَآ إِنَّكَ رَءُوفٌ رَّحِيمٌ.

Arabic

Rabbana ghfir lana wa li-ikhwanina allatheena sabaquna bil-eemani wa la taj'al fi quloobina ghillan lilladheena amanu Rabbana innaka Ra'ufun Rahim.

Phonetic transcription

O Allah, forgive us and our brothers who preceded us in faith and put not in our hearts any resentment toward those who have believed. Our Lord, indeed You are Kind and Merciful.

English

Reference: Surat Al-Hashr (59:10)

## 171 PRAYER FOR BLESSING A MARRIAGE

بَارَكَ اللَّهُ لَكَ وَبَارَكَ عَلَيْكَ وَجَمَعَ بَيْنَكُمَا فِي الْخَيْرِ.

Arabic

Bāraka llāhu lak, wa bāraka `alayk, wa jama`a baynakumā fī lkhayr.

Phonetic transcription

May Allah bless you and shower His blessings upon you, and may He bring you together in goodness.

English

Reference: Abu Dawud, Ibn Majah and At-Tirmidhi

## 172 PRAYER FOR THE SUPPORT OF ALL THE RIGHTEOUS

جعلَ اللهُ عليكُم صلاةَ قَومٍ أبرارٍ، لَيسوا بِظَلَمَةٍ ولا فُجَّارٍ، يقومونَ اللَّيلَ ويصومونَ النَّهارَ.

Arabic

Ja'al Llahu 'alayhi salat qawm 'abrar laysuu bidhalama wala fujar, yaqumun llayla, wa yasumun nnahara.

Phonetic transcription

May Allah bless him with the blessing of those who are pious, who are neither unjust nor corrupt, and who stand at night in prayer and fast in the day.

English

Reference: Al-Adab Al-Mufrad 631

## 173 PRAYER FOR SOMEONE WHOSE FAITH IS WEAK

آمنتُ باللهِ ورُسُلِه.

Arabic

Falyaqul amantu billahi warusulihi.

So let him say, I have believed in Allah and His messengers.

Reference: Muslim, 1/119-20

Phonetic transcription

English

## 174 PRAYER FOR WELFARE AND WEALTH FOR OTHERS

اللَّهُمَّ ارْزُقْهُ مَالًا وَوَلَدًا وَبَارِكْ لَهُ فِيهِ.

Arabic

Allahuma rzuqhu malan wa waladan wabarik lahu fih.

O Allah! Give him property and children and bless him.

Reference: Sahih al-Bukhari 1982

Phonetic transcription

English

## 175 PRAYER TO PUNISH OR REWARD THOSE IN POWER

اللَّهُمَّ مَنْ وَلِيَ مِنْ أَمْرِ أُمَّتِي شَيْئًا فَشَقَّ عَلَيْهِمْ فَاشْقُقْ عَلَيْهِ وَمَنْ وَلِيَ مِنْ أَمْرِ أُمَّتِي شَيْئًا فَرَفَقَ بِهِمْ فَارْفُقْ بِهِ.

Arabic

Allahuma man walia min 'amra 'umati shay'an fashaqa 'layhim fashquq 'alayh wa man walia min 'amri 'umati shay'an farafaqa bihim farfuq bihi.

O Allah, whoever has authority over my people and is harsh with them, be harsh with him, and whoever has authority over my people and is kind to them, be kind to him!

Reference: Mishkat al-Masabih 3689

Phonetic transcription

English

# 176 PRAYER FOR FORGIVENESS FOR A DYING PERSON

اللَّهُمَّ اغْفِرْ لَهُ وَأَعْقِبْنَا عُقْبَى صَالِحَةً.

Arabic

Allahumma ighfir lahu wa aqibna 'uqba saliha.

O Allah forgive him, and give us something good in exchange.

Phonetic transcription

Reference: Sunan Abi Dawud 3115

English

# 177 PRAYER FOR LENIENCY WITH THE DEBTORS

بَارَكَ اللَّهُ لَكَ فِي أَهْلِكَ وَمَالِكَ إِنَّمَا جَزَاءُ السَّلَفِ الْوَفَاءُ وَالْحَمْدُ.

Arabic

Baraka llahu laka fi ahlik wa mālik, innamā jazā'u sālifi al-hamdu wa l-ada'.

May Allah bless You in Your family and Your wealth, surely the reward for a loan is praise and returning (what was borrowed).

Phonetic transcription

Reference: An-Nasa'i, 'Amalul-Yawm wal-Laylah p. 300, Ibn Majah 2/809

English

# 178 PRAYER FOR PROTECTION OF A TRAVELLER

اللَّهُمَّ اطْوِ لَهُ الْأَرْضَ وَهَوِّنْ عَلَيْهِ السَّفَرَ.

Arabic

Allahumma twi lahu al-ard wa hawin 'alayhi safar.

O Allah, make near for him the distance, and ease for him the journey.

Phonetic transcription

Reference: Jami' at Tirmidhi 3445

English

## 179 PRAYER TO BLESS A PLACE OR CITY

رَبِّ ٱجْعَلْ هَٰذَا بَلَدًا ءَامِنًا وَٱرْزُقْ أَهْلَهُۥ مِنَ ٱلثَّمَرَٰتِ مَنْ ءَامَنَ مِنْهُم بِٱللَّهِ وَٱلْيَوْمِ ٱلْءَاخِرِ.

Arabic

Rabbi ij'al haadha baladan aaminan warzuq ahlahu mina thamarati man amana minhum billahi wa lyawmi l-akhir.

Phonetic transcription

Reference: Surat Al-Baqarah (2:126)

My Lord, make this city secure and provide its people with fruits for those who believe in Allah and the Hereafter.

English

## 180 PRAYER FOR THE SAFETY OF A PLACE

رَبِّ ٱجْعَلْ هَٰذَا ٱلْبَلَدَ ءَامِنًا وَٱجْنُبْنِي وَبَنِيَّ أَن نَّعْبُدَ ٱلْأَصْنَامَ.

Arabic

Rabbi j'al hadha lbald aaminan wajnubni wabaniyya an na'buda lasnam.

Phonetic transcription

Reference: Surat Ibrahim (14:35)

O Allah, make this city secure and keep me and my sons away from worshiping idols.

English

## 181 PRAYER TO BLESS SOMEONE WEARING NEW CLOTHES

تُبْلِي وَيُخْلِفُ اللَّهُ تَعَالَى.

Arabic

Tublī wa yukhlifu llāhu ta`ālā.

Phonetic transcription

Reference: Abu Dawud 4/41

May Allah replace it when it is worn out.

English

## 182 PRAYER TO BLESS A HOST

اللَّهمَّ أَطْعِمْ مَنْ أَطْعَمَنِي، وَاسْقِ مَنْ سَقَانِي.

Arabic

Allāhumma aṭ`im man aṭ`amanī wasqi man saqānī.

Phonetic transcription

Reference: Muslim 3/126

O Allah, feed those who have fed me, and give drink to those who have given me drink.

English

## 183 PRAYER FOR THE WELFARE OF A GUEST

أَفْطَرَ عِنْدَكُمُ الصَّائِمُونَ وَأَكَلَ طَعَامَكُمُ الأَبْرَارُ وَصَلَّتْ عَلَيْكُمُ الْمَلَائِكَةُ.

Arabic

Afṭara `indakumu ṣā'imūna, wa akala ṭa`āmakumu 'l'abrār, wa ṣallat `alaykumu lmalā'ikah.

Phonetic transcription

Reference: Abu Dawud 3/367

May the fasting break their fast in your house, the righteous partake of your food, and the angels send blessings upon you.

English

## 184 PRAYER FOR THE WELFARE OF A PHILANTHROPIST

جَزَاكَ اللَّهُ خَيْرًا.

Arabic

Jazāka llāhu khayran.

Phonetic transcription

Reference: At-Tirmidhi (no. 2035)

May Allah reward you with goodness.

English

## 185 PRAYER FOR THE WELFARE OF A LOVED ONE

- إِنِّي أُحِبُّكَ فِي اللهِ!

- أَحَبَّكَ الَّذِي أَحْبَبْتَنِي لَهُ!

Arabic

- 'uhibuka fi llahi!

- Aḥabbaka 'lladhī aḥbabtanī lah.

Phonetic transcription

Reference: Abu Dawud 4/333

- I love you for the sake of Allah

- May He for Whose sake You love me, love You.

English

## 186 PRAYER FOR MERCY FOR THE PARENTS

رَّبِّ ٱرْحَمْهُمَا كَمَا رَبَّيَانِي صَغِيرًا.

Arabic

Rabbi rhamhuma kama rabbayani sagheera.

Phonetic transcription

Reference: Surat Al-Isra (17:24)

O Alalh, Have mercy upon them as they brought me up when I was small.

English

## 187 PRAYER TO BE KIND TO THE PARENTS AND GUESTS

رَّبِّ ٱغْفِرْ لِي وَلِوَٰلِدَيَّ وَلِمَن دَخَلَ بَيْتِيَ مُؤْمِنًا وَلِلْمُؤْمِنِينَ وَٱلْمُؤْمِنَٰتِ.

Arabic

Rabbi ghfir li wa liwalidayya waliman dakhala baytiya muminan wa li lmuminina wa lmuminati.

Phonetic transcription

Reference: Surat Nuh 71:28

O Allah, forgive me, my parents, and whoever enters my house as believers, and forgive the believing men and women.

English

# 188 PRAYER FOR FAVOR WHEN SOMEONE SNEEZES

- الْحَمْدُ لِلَّهِ!

- يَرْحَمُكَ اللَّهُ!

- يَهْدِيكُمُ اللَّهُ وَيُصْلِحُ بَالَكُمْ!

Arabic

- Al-hamdu lillah
- Yarhamuka llah
- Yahdikumu llahu wa yuslihu balakum

Phonetic transcription

-Praise be to Allah.
-May Allah have mercy on you.
-May Allah guide you and rectify your affairs.

English

Reference: Al-Bukhari 7/125

# 189 PRAYER FOR THE WELL-BEING OF THE FAMILY IN THIS WORLD AND IN THE HEREAFTER

رَبَّنَآ ءَاتِنَا فِي ٱلدُّنْيَا حَسَنَةً وَفِي ٱلْأَخِرَةِ حَسَنَةً وَقِنَا عَذَابَ ٱلنَّارِ.

Arabic

Rabbana atina fi ddunya hasanah wa fi lakhirati hasanah wa qina 'adhaba an-nar.

Phonetic transcription

O Allah, give us the good of this world and the good of the Hereafter, and save us from the punishment of Hell.

English

Reference: Surat Al-Baqarah (2:201)

# 190 PRAYER TO BLESS A FAMILY WITH A NEWBORN

بَارَكَ اللَّهُ لَكَ فِي الـمَوْهُوبِ لَكَ، وَشَكَرْتَ الوَاهِبَ، وبَلَغَ أَشُدَّهُ، وَرُزِقْتَ بِرَّهُ.

Arabic

Bāraka llāhu laka fi 'l-mawhūbi lak, wa shakarta 'l-wāhib, wa balagha ashuddah, wa ruziqta birrah.

Phonetic transcription

May Allah bless the child He has given you, and may you show gratitude to Allah. May he reach its full potential, and may you be blessed with goodness.

English

Reference: An-Nawawi, Kitdbul-'Athkarp

# Prayers for healing and health

## 191 PRAYER TO HEAL A SICK PERSON

أَسْأَلُ اللَّهَ الْعَظِيمَ رَبَّ الْعَرْشِ الْعَظِيمِ أَنْ يَشْفِيَكَ.

Arabic

As'alu llāha 'l-`adīma rabba 'l-`arshi l-`adīmi an yashfik.

I ask Almighty Allah, the Lord of the mighty Throne, to heal you.

Phonetic transcription

Reference: At-Tirmidhi, Abu Dawud. See also Al-Albani, Sahih At-Tirmidhi 2/210 and Sahihul-Jami' As-Saghir 5/180

English

## 192 PRAYER FOR REGENERATION AND RETRIBUTION

اللهم أَصلِح لِـي سمعِي وبصرِي واجعلهما الوارِثَين مِني، وانصرنِي على من ظَلَمنِي، وأَرنِي مِنه ثَأري.

Arabic

Allahuma 'aslih li sam'i wa basari, waj'alhuma alwarithayni mini, wansurni 'ala man dalamani, wa arini minh thari.

O Allah, let my hearing and sight be sound and make them remain sound until I die. Turn away from me the one who wrongs me and give me revenge on him.

Phonetic transcription

Reference: Al-Adab Al-Mufrad 649

English

## 193 PRAYER FOR A HEALTHY BODY AND MIND

اللَّهُمَّ عَافِنِي فِي بَدَنِي اللَّهُمَّ عَافِنِي فِي سَمْعِي اللَّهُمَّ عَافِنِي بَصَرِي لاَ إِلَهَ إِلاَّ أَنْتَ، اللَّهُمَّ إِنِّي أَعُوذُ بِكَ مِنَ الْكُفْرِ وَالْفَقْرِ اللَّهُمَّ إِنِّي أَعُوذُ بِكَ مِنْ عَذَابِ الْقَبْرِ لاَ إِلَهَ إِلاَّ أَنْتَ.

Arabic

Allahumma 'afini fi badani, Allahumma 'afini fi sam'i, Allahumma 'afini fi basari. La ilaha illa Anta. Allahumma inni a'udhu bika min al-kufr wa l-faqr. Allahumma inni a'udhu bika min 'adhabi al-qabr. La ilaha illa Anta.

O Allah, make me healthy in my body. O Allah, make me healthy in my hearing. O Allah, make me healthy in my sight. There is no god but You. 'O Allah, I seek refuge in You from disbelief and poverty. O Allah, I seek refuge in You from the torment of the grave. There is no god but You.

Phonetic transcription

Reference: Al-Adab Al-Mufrad 701

English

## 194 PRAYER FOR A SICK PERSON

لَا بَأْسَ عَلَيْكَ، طَهُورٌ إِنْ شَاءَ اللَّهُ.

Arabic

La basa 'alaika, tahoorun in sha' Allah.

Do not worry, it will be a purification for You, Allah willing.

Phonetic transcription

Reference: Al-Bukhari, cf. Al-Asqalani Fathul-Bari 10/118

English

## 195 PRAYER TO EASE THE PAIN

أَعُوذُ بِاللَّهِ وَقُدْرَتِهِ مِنْ شَرِّ مَا أَجِدُ وَأُحَاذِرُ.

Arabic

A'udhu biazatillahi wa qudratihi min sharri ma ajidu wa ahadhir.

I seek refuge in the might and power of Allah from the evil of what I feel and apprehend.

Phonetic transcription

Reference: Riyad as-Salihin 905

English

## 196 PRAYER FOR FULL RECOVERY

اللَّهُمَّ رَبَّ النَّاس، أَذْهِبِ البأسَ، اشْفِ أنت الشافي، لا شِفَاءَ إِلَّا شِفَاؤُكَ، شِفَاءً لا يُغَادِرُ سَقَمًا.

Arabic

Allahumma Rabba nasi, adhhibi lba'sa, washfi, antashfi, la shifa'a illa shifa'uka, shifaan la yughadiru saqaman.

O Allah, Lord of mankind, remove the affliction and heal, for You are the Healer, and there is no healing except Your healing, a healing that leaves no disease.

Phonetic transcription

Reference: Muslim 4/1721

English

# 197 PRAYER TO HEAL CHARACTER WEAKNESSES

اللَّهُمَّ إِنِّي أَعُوذُ بِكَ مِنْ شَرِّ سَمْعِي، وَمِنْ شَرِّ بَصَرِي، وَمِنْ شَرِّ لِسَانِي، وَمِنْ شَرِّ قَلْبِي، وَمِنْ شَرِّ مَنِيِّي.

Arabic

Allāhumma innī a`ūdhu bika min sharri sam`ī wa min sharri baṣarī, wa min sharri lisānī, wa min sharri qalbī, wa min sharri maniyī.

O Allah, I seek refuge in You from the evil of my hearing, the evil of my sight, the evil of my tongue, the evil of my heart, and the evil of my lust.

Phonetic transcription

Reference: Jami' at-Tirmidhi 3492

English

# 198 PRAYER FOR PROTECTION FROM ALL DISEASES

اللَّهُمَّ إِنِّي أَعُوذُ بِكَ مِنَ الْبَرَصِ، وَالْجُنُونِ، وَالْجُذَامِ، وَمِنْ سَيِّئِ الأَسْقَامِ.

Arabic

Allahumma inni a'udhu bika mina ljununi wa ljudhami, wa lbarasi wa sayy'l l-asqami.

O Allah, I seek refuge in You from leucoderma, madness, leprosy, and all evil diseases.

Phonetic transcription

Reference: Sunan an-Nasa'i 5493

English

# 199 PRAYER FOR HELP AND HEALING

ربَّنا اللهُ الذي في السَّماءِ تقدَّسَ اسمُكَ أمرُكَ في السَّماءِ والأرضِ كما رحمتُكَ في السَّماءِ فاجعلْ رحمتَكَ في الأرضِ اغفرْ لنا حُوبَنا وخطايانا أنتَ ربُّ الطَّيِّبين أنزِلْ رحمةً وشفاءً من شفائِكَ على هذا الوجعِ فيبرأَ.

Arabic

Rabana allahu aladhi fi sama' taqadasa smak 'amraka fi sama'i wa l'ard kama rahamatuka fi sama'i ijaal rahmataka fi l'ardi ighfir lana hawbana wa khatayana 'anta rabu ltayibina 'anzil rahmatan min rahmatika wa shifa'an min shifayika alaa hadha lwajae fayabra.

Our Lord, Allah, who is in heaven, hallowed be Your name. Your command is in heaven and the earth. As Your mercy is in heaven, Make Your mercy on earth. Forgive us our sins and our transgressions. You are the Lord of the virtuous. Send down mercy and healing from You upon this pain, so it may be cured.

Reference: Sunan Abi Daud -Mishkat al-Masabih 1555

Phonetic transcription

English

# 200 PRAYER FOR PROTECTION FROM WEAKNESS AND DISEASE

اللَّهُمَّ عَافِنِي فِي بَدَنِي اللَّهُمَّ عَافِنِي فِي سَمْعِي اللَّهُمَّ عَافِنِي بَصَرِيف. لاَ إِلَهَ إِلاَّ أَنْتَ. اللَّهمَّ إِنِّي أَعوذُ
بكَ منَ الكُفرِ والفقرِ، اللَّهمَّ إِنِّي أَعوذُ بِكَ مِن عَذابِ القَبرِ، إلا إِلهَ إِلَّا أنتَ.

Arabic

Allahumma, afini fee badani. Allahumma, afini fee sam'e. Allahumma, afini fee basari. La ilaha illa Anta. Allahumma, inni a'udhu bika min al-kufr wal-faqr. Allahumma, inni a'udhu bika min 'adhabi l-qabr. La ilaha illa Anta.

Phonetic transcription

Reference: Al-Adab Al-Mufrad 701

O Allah, grant me health in my body, protect my hearing, and preserve my sight. There is no god but You. O Allah, I seek refuge in You from disbelief and poverty. O Allah, I seek refuge in You from the torment of the grave. There is no god but You.

English

# Prayers for the deceased

## 201 PRAYER FOR FORGIVENESS FOR THE DECEASED PERSON AND FOR THE SURVIVORS

اللَّهُمَّ اغْفِرْ لِحَيِّنَا وَمَيِّتِنَا، وَشَاهِدِنَا وَغَائِبِنَا، وَصَغِيرِنَا وَذَكَبِيرِنَا، وَذَكَرِنَا وَأُنْثَانَا، اللَّهُمَّهُ مَنْ أَحْيَيْتَهُ مِنَّا
فَأَحْيِهِ عَلَى الْإِسْلَامِ، وَمَنْ تَوَفَّيْتَهُ مِنَّا فَتَوَفَّهُ عَلَى الْإِيمَانِ، اللَّهُمَّا أَجْرَهُ، وَلَا تُضِلَّنَا بَعْدَهُ.

Arabic

Allāhumma ghfir liḥayyinā, wa mayyitinā, wa shāhidinā, wa ghā'ibinā, wa ṣaghīrinā wa kabīrinā, wa dhakarinā wa unthānā. Allāhumma man aḥyaytahu minnā fa aḥyihi `ala l-Islām, wa man tawaffaytahu minnā fatawaffahu `ala l-īmān, Allāhumma lā taḥrimnā ajrahu wa lā tuḍillanā ba`dahu.

O Allah forgive our living and our dead, those who are with us and those who are absent, our Young and old, our male and female. O Allah, whoever You keep alive from among us, let them live according to Islam, and whoever You cause to die from among us, let them die in faith. O Allah, do not deprive us of the reward for this, and do not lead us astray after their passing.

Reference: Ibn Majah 1/480, Ahmad 2/368

Phonetic transcription

English

## 202 PRAYER FOR A DECEASED PERSON TO GO TO PARADISE

اللَّهُمَّ صَلِّ عَلَيْهِ، وَاغْفِرْ لَهُ وَارْحَمْهُ، وَعَافِهِ وَاعْفُ عَنْهُ، وَاغْسِلْهُ بِمَاءٍ وَثَلْجٍ وَبَرَدٍ، وَنَقِّهِ مِنَ الذُّنُوبِه
وَالْخَطَايَا كَمَا يُنَقَّى ;الثَّوْبُ الْأَبْيَضُ مِنَ الدَّنَسِ، وَأَبْدِلْهُ بِدَارِهِ دَارًا خَيْرًا مِنْ دَارِهِ، وَأَهْلًا خَيْرًا مِنْ
أَهْلِهِ، وَقِهِ فِتْنَةَ الْقَبْرِ وَعَذَابَ النَّارِ!

Arabic

Allahumma salli 'alayhi waghfir lahu wa rhamhu, wa 'afihi wa'fu 'anhu, wa ghsilhu bi ma'in wa thaljin wa baradin, wa naqqihi mina dhunubi wal-khataya kama yunaqqa thawbu l-abyadu mina danas, wa abdilhu bi darihi daran khayran min darihi, wa ahlan khayran min ahlili, wa qihi fitnata l-qabri wa 'adhaba nnar.

O Allah, send blessing upon him, forgive him, have mercy on him, keep him safe and sound, and pardon him; wash him with water and snow and hail, and cleanse him of sins just as a white garment is cleansed of dirt. Give him in exchange for his house that is better than his house, and a family that is better than his family. Protect him from the trial of the grave and the torment of Hell.

Reference: Sunan Ibn Majah 1500

Phonetic transcription

English

## 203 PRAYER FOR SUCCOUR AT A FUNERAL

اَللَّهمَّ أنتَ ربُّها وأنت خلقتَها وأنت هديتَها للإسلامِ وأنت قبضتَ رُوحَها أنت أعلمُ بسِرِّها وعلانيَتِها
جِئنا شُفعاءُ فاغفِرْ لها!

Arabic

Allahumma anta rabbuha wa anta khalaqtaha wa anta hadaytaha lil-islami wa anta qabadta rooḥaha wa anta a'lamu bi sirriha wa 'alaniyatiha. Ji'nā shufa'a'u, faghfir laha.

O Allah, You are her Lord, and You created her, and You guided her to Islam, and You took her soul, and You know her secrets and public affairs. We have come as intercessors, so forgive her sins.

Reference: Riyad as-Salihin 938

Phonetic transcription

English

## 204 PRAYER AFTER A BURIAL

اللَّهمَّ فاغفر لهُ اللَّهمَّ ثبته.

Arabic

Allāhumma ghfir lah Allāhumma thabbit'h.

O Allah, forgive him. O Allah, grant him steadfastness.

Reference: Abu Dawud 3/315

Phonetic transcription

English

## 205 PRAYER FOR BLESSINGS AND MERCY FOR A DECEASED PERSON

اللَّهُمَّ اغْفِرْ له وَارْحَمْهُ، وَعَافِهِ وَاعْفُ عنْه، وَأَكْرِمْ نُزُلَهُ، وَوَسِّعْ مُدْخَلَهُ، وَاغْسِلْهُ بالمَاءِ وَالْبَرَد، وَالْبَرَد، وَنَقِّهِ مِنَ الخَطَايَا كما نَقَّيْتَ الثَّوْبَ الأبْيَضَ مِنَ الدَّنَسِ، وَأَبْدِلْهُ دَارًا خَيْرًا مِن دَارِهِ، وَأَهْلًا خَيْرًا مِن أَهْلِهِ، وَزَوْجًا خَيْرًا مِن زَوْجِهِ، وَأَدْخِلْهُ الجَنَّةَ، وَأَعِذْهُ مِن عَذَابِ القَبْرِ، أَوْ مِن عَذَابِ النَّارِ .

Arabic

Allāhumma ghfir lahu wa rḥamh wa `āfih wa`fu `anh wa akrim nuzulah wa wassi` mudkhalah wa ghsilhu bi lmā'i wa thalji wa lbarad wa naqqihi mina lkhaṭāyā kamā naqqayta thawba l-abyaḍa mina danas wa abdilhu dāran khayran min dārih wa ahlan khayran min ahlih wa zawjan khayran min zawjih wa adkhilhu l-jannah wa a`idhhu min `adhābi 'l-qabri aw `adhābi nnār.

O Allah, forgive him, have mercy on him, and grant him well-being and forgiveness. Honor his resting place, widen his entrance, wash him with water, snow, and ice, purify him from sins as You purify the white garment from impurity. Replace his home with a better home, and his family with a better family. Grant him a better spouse and admit him to Paradise. Protect him from the torment of the grave and the torment of the Fire.

Reference: Muslim 2/663

Phonetic transcription

English

## 206 PRAYER TO ALLAH FOR A DECEASED CHILD AND ITS PARENTS

اللَّهُمَّ اجْعَلْهُ فَرَطًا لِوَالِدَيْهِ، وَذُخْرًا وَسَلَفًا وَأَجْرًا، اللَّهُمَّ ثَقِّلْ بِهِ مَوَازِينَهُمَا، وَأَعْظِمْ بِهِ أُجُورَهُمَا، اللَّهُمَّ اجْعَلْهُ فِي كَفَالَةِ إِبْرَاهِيمَ وَأَلْحِقْهُ بِصَالِحِ سَلَفِ الْمُؤْمِنِينَ، وَأَجِرْهُ بِرَحْمَتِك مِنْ عَذَابِ الْجَحِيمِ، وَأَبْدِلْهُ دَارًا خَيْرًا مِنْ دَارِهِ، وَأَهْلًا خَيْرًا مِنْ أَهْلِهِ، اللَّهُمَّ اغْفِرْ لِأَسْلَافِنَا وَأَفْرَاطِنَا وَمَنْ سَبَقَنَا بِالْإِيمَانِ.

Arabic

Allahumma aj'alhu faratan li walidayhi, wadukhran wasalafan wa ajran. Allahumma thaqil bihi mawazinahuma, wa a'dhim bihi ujoorahuma. Allahumma j'alhu fi kafaalati Ibrahima wa alhiqhu bissalihi salafi l-mu'minin. Wa ajirhu bi rahmatika min 'adhabi l-jahim. Wa abdilhu daraan khayran min darih, wa ahlan khayran min ahlih. Allahumma ghfir li aslafina wa afraatina wa man sabaqana bi l-iman.

O Allah, make him a source of pride for his parents, a treasure, a forerunner, and a reward. O Allah, make him weigh heavy in their scales, and magnify their rewards through him. O Allah, place him under the care of Abraham and join him with the righteous predecessors among the believers. Grant him refuge through Your mercy from the punishment of Hell. Replace his home with a better home and his family with a better family. O Allah, forgive our predecessors, our successors, and those who precede us in faith.

Reference: Ibn Qudamah, Al-Mughni 3/416 and Ad-Duroosul-Muhimmah li-Aammatil-Ummah, pg. 15, by Shaikh 'Abdul-'Aziz bin Baz

Phonetic transcription

English

## 207 PRAYER FOR FORGIVENESS FOR A DECEASED & PRAYER FOR CONSOLATION

اللهُـمِّ اغْفِـرْ لِـفلان (باسـمه) وَارْفَعْ دَرَجَتَـهُ في المَهْـدِيـن، وَاخْـلُفْـهُ في عَقِـبِهِ في الغابِـرين، وَاغْفِـرْ لَنـا وَلَـهُ يا رَبَّ العـالَـمين، وَافْسَـحْ لَهُ في قَبْـرِهِ وَنَـوِّرْ لَهُ فيه .

Arabic

Allāhumma'ghfir li (name of the person) warfa` darajatahu fi l-mahdiyyīn, wakhlufhu fī `aqibihi fi 'l-ghābirīn, wagh'fir lanā wa lahu yā Rabba 'l-`ālamīn, wafsaḥ lahu fī qabrihi wa nawwir lahu fīh.

O Allah, forgive [name of the person] and elevate him among the guided ones. Send him along the path of those who came before, and forgive him and us. O Lord of the worlds, enlarge for him his grave, and shed light for him.

Reference: Muslim 2/634

Phonetic transcription

English

## 208 PRAYER FOR THE REST IN PEACE OF THE DECEASED

السَّلامُ عَلَيْكُم أَهلَ الدِّيارِ منَ المؤمنينَ والمسلمينَ، وإنَّا إن شاءَ اللَّهُ بِكم لاحقونَ، نسألُ اللَّهَ لنا ولَكمُ العافيةَ.

Arabic

Assalāmu `alaykum ahla ddiyāri mina l-mu'minīna wa l-muslimīn, wa innā in shā' allāhu bikum lāḥiqūn nas'alu llāha lanā wa lakumu l'āfiyah.

Peace be upon you, O residents of these abodes, from among the believers and Muslims. Surely, we are, by the will of Allah, soon to follow you. We ask Allah for well-being for us and for you.

Reference: Muslim 2/671, Ibn Majah 1/494, the portion brackets is from Muslim 2/671

Phonetic transcription

English

# Prayers for different times of the day

## 209 PRAYER FOR GOODNESS IN THE MORNING AND IN THE EVENING

اللَّهُمَّ إِنِّي أَسْأَلُكَ الْعَافِيَةَ فِي الدُّنْيَا وَالآخِرَةِ اللَّهُمَّ إِنِّي أَسْأَلُكَ الْعَفْوَ وَالْعَافِيَةَ فِي دِينِي وَدُنْيَايَ وَأَهْلِي
وَمَالِي. اللَّهُمَّ اسْتُرْ عَوْرَاتِي وَآمِنْ رَوْعَاتِي. اللَّهُمَّ احْفَظْنِي مِنْ بَيْنِ يَدَىَّ وَمِنْ خَلْفِي وَعَنْ يَمِينِي وَمِنْ
فَوْقِي وَأَعُوذُ بِعَظَمَتِكَ أُغْتَالَ مِنْ تَحْتِي.

Arabic

Allāhumma innī as'aluka 'l-`afwa wal-`āfiyah fid-dunyā wa l-ākhirah, Allāhumma innī as'aluka 'l-`afwa wal-`āfiyah fī dīnī wa dunyāya, wa ahlī, wa mālī, Allāhumma stur `awrātī, wa āmin raw`ātī, Allāhumma ḥfadnī min bayni yadayya, wa min khalfī, wa `an yamīnī, wa `an shimālī, wa min fawqī, wa a`ūdhu bi`aẓamatika an 'ughtāla min taḥtī.

O Allah, I ask You for well-being in this world and the Hereafter. O Allah, I ask You for forgiveness and well-being in my religion, my worldly life, my family, and my wealth. O Allah, conceal my faults and calm my fears. O Allah, protect me from in front, from behind, from my right, from my left, and from above. I seek refuge in Your greatness that I may be attacked from beneath.

Reference: Sahih Ibn Majah 2/332 and Abu Dawud

Phonetic transcription

English

## 210 PRAYER FOR FORGIVENESS OF SINS (MORNING AND EVENING)

اللَّهُمَّ أَنْتَ رَبِّي لَا إِلَهَ إِلَّا أَنْتَ، خَلَقْتَنِي وَأَنَا عَبْدُكَ، وَأَنَا عَلَى عَهْدِكَ مَا اسْتَطَعْتُ، أَعُوذُ بِكَ مِنْ شَرِّ
مَا صَنَعْتُ، أَبُوءُ لَكَ بِنِعْمَتِكَ عَلَيَّ، وَأَبُوءُ بِذَنْبِي فَاغْفِر لِي فَإِنَّهُ لَا يَغْفِرُ الذُّنُوبَ إِلَّا أَنْتَ.

Arabic

Allāhumma anta Rabbī lā ilāha illā ant, khalaqtanī wa anā `abduk, wa anā `alā `ahdika wa wa`dika mastaṭa`t, a`ūdhu bika min sharri mā ṣana`t, abū'u laka bi ni`matika `alaya, wa abū'u bidhanbī faghfir lī fa'innahu lā yaghfiru dhunūba illā anta.

O Allah, You are my Lord, there is no god but You. You created me and I am Your servant. I am upon Your covenant and promise as much as I can. I seek refuge in You from the evil of what I have done. I acknowledge Your blessings upon me, and I confess my sins. So forgive me, as no one forgives sins except You.

Phonetic transcription

Reference: Al-Bukhari 7/150. Other reports are in An-Nasa'i and At-Tirmidhi

English

## 211 PRAYER UPON WAKING UP FROM SLEEP

الْحَمْدُ للهِ الَّذِي عَافَانِي فِي جَسَدِي، وَرَدَّ عَلَيَّ رُوحِي، وَأَذِنَ لِي بِذِكْرِهِ.

Arabic

Al-ḥamdu lillāhi ladhī `āfānī fī jasadī, wa radda `alayya rūḥī, wa 'adhina lī bidhikrih.

All praise be to Allah, who granted me health in my body, returned my soul to me, and allowed me to remember Him.

Phonetic transcription

Reference: At-Tirmidhi 5/473

English

# 212 PRAYER FOR PROTECTION (BEFORE BEDTIME)

اللَّهُمَّ خَلَقْتَ نَفْسِي وَأَنْتَ تَوَفَّاهَا لَكَ مَمَاتُهَا وَمَحْيَاهَا إِنْ أَحْيَيْتَهَا فَاحْفَظْهَا وَإِنْ أَمَتَّهَا فَاغْفِرْ لَهَا اللَّهُمَّ إِنِّي أَسْأَلُكَ الْعَافِيَةَ.

Arabic

Allāhumma khalagta nafsi wa-anta tawaffāhā laka mamātuhā wa-mahyāhā in ahyaytahā fa-hfathhā wa-in amattahā fa-ghfir la-hā llāhumma inni as'aluka l-"āfiya.

Phonetic transcription

Reference: Muslim 4/2083 and Ahmad 2/79

O Allah, You created my soul, and when its time comes, You take it back. Whether You let it live or cause it to die. If You let it live, preserve it, and if You cause it to die, forgive it. O Allah, I ask You for well-being.

English

# 213 PRAYER FOR REFUGE (BEFORE BEDTIME)

اللَّهُمَّ رَبَّ السَّمَاوَاتِ وَرَبَّ الْأَرْضِ وَرَبَّ الْعَرْشِ الْعَظِيمِ رَبَّنَا وَرَبَّ كُلِّ شَيْءٍ فَالِقَ الْحَبِّ وَالنَّوَى وَمُنْزِلَ التَّوْرَاةِ وَالْإِنْجِيلِ وَالْفُرْقَانِ أَعُوذُ بِكَ مِنْ شَرِّ كُلِّ شَيْءٍ أَنْتَ آخِذٌ بِنَاصِيَتِهِ اللَّهُمَّ أَنْتَ الْأَوَّلُ فَلَيْسَ قَبْلَكَ شَيْءٌ وَأَنْتَ الْآخِرُ فَلَيْسَ بَعْدَكَ شَيْءٌ وَأَنْتَ الظَّاهِرُ فَلَيْسَ فَوْقَكَ شَيْءٌ وَأَنْتَ الْبَاطِنُ فَلَيْسَ دُونَكَ شَيْءٌ اقْضِ عَنَّا الدَّيْنَ وَأَغْنِنَا مِنَ الْفَقْرِ.

Arabic

Allahumma rabbas-samawati warabbal-ardi warabbal-arshi al-azheem, rabbana wa rabbu kulli shay, faliqal-habb wan-nawa, munzilat-tawrati wal-injili wal-furqani, a'udhu bika min sharri kulli shay, anta akhizu binasiyatihi. Allahumma anta al-awwalu, falaysa qablaka shay, wa anta al-akhiru, falaysa ba'daka shay, wa anta adh-dhahiru, falaysa fawqaka shay, wa anta al-batinu, falaysa doonaka shay. Iqdi annad-dayna wa aghninamina al-faqri.

Phonetic transcription

Reference: Sahih Muslim 2713, Jami' at-Tirmidhi 3481

O Allah, Lord of the heavens and the earth, and Lord of the mighty throne, our Lord and the Lord of everything, Splitter of the seed and the date stone, Revealer of the Torah, the Gospel, and the Quran, I seek refuge with You from the evil of everything You controle. O Allah, You are the First, and there is nothing before You, and You are the Last, and there is nothing after You. You are the Manifest, and there is nothing above You, and You are the Hidden, and there is nothing beyond You. Settle our debt, and free us from poverty.

English

# 214 PRAYER FOR PROTECTION FROM THE DEVIL (BEFORE BEDTIME)

بِسْمِ اللهِ وَضَعْتُ جَنْبِي اللَّهُمَّ اغْفِرْ لِي ذَنْبِي وَأَخْسِئْ شَيْطَانِي وَفُكَّ رِهَانِي وَاجْعَلْنِي فِي النَّدِيِّ الأَعْلَى.

Arabic

Bism llahi wadaatu janby allahuma ghfir li dhanbi wa khsa` shaytani wa fuka rihani wa j`alni fi nnadii ala'laa.

Phonetic transcription

Reference: Sunan Abu Dawud 5054

In the name of Allah, I lay down for sleep. O Allah, forgive my sins, drive away my devil, and unshackle my bonds. Place me in the highest level of paradise.

English

## 215 PRAYER FOR MERCY (BEFORE BEDTIME)

اللَّهُمَّ قِنِي عَذَابَكَ يَوْمَ تَبْعَثُ عِبَادَكَ.

Arabic

Allāhumma qinī `adhābaka yawma tab`athu `ibādak.

O Allah, save me from Your punishment on the Day that You resurrect Your servants.

Phonetic transcription

Reference: Abu Dawud 4/311

English

## 216 PRAYER FOR A FIRM BELIEF AT THE BEGINNING OF THE DAY

اللَّهُمَّ إِنِّي أَصْبَحْتُ أُشْهِدُكَ وَأُشْهِدُ حَمَلَةَ عَرْشِكَ، وَمَلَائِكَتَكَ وَجَمِيعَ خَلْقِكَ، أَنَّكَ أَنْتَ اللهُ لَا إِلَّا أَنْتَ وَحْدَكَ لَا شَرِيكَ لَكَ، وَأَنَا عَبْدُكَ وَرَسُولُكَ.

Arabic

Allahuma 'iniy 'asbahtu 'ushhiduk wa'ushhid hamalat earshika, wamala'ikatak wajamia khalqika, 'anaka 'anta llahu la 'ilaha 'illa 'anta wahdak la sharika laka, wa 'ana muhamadan eabduka wa rasuluka.

O Allah, I bear You witness this morning, and I bear witness to the bearers of Your Throne, Your angels, and all Your creation, that You are Allah, there is no god but You alone, with no partner, and that Muhammad is Your servant and Your Messenger.

Phonetic transcription

Reference: Sunan Abi Dawud 5078

English

## 217 PRAYER FOR REGARD (BEFORE BEDTIME)

اللَّهُمَّ باسْمِكَ أَحْيَا وأَمُوتُ.

Arabic

Allāhumma bismika amūtu wa aḥyā.

O Allah, by Your Name I live and die.

Phonetic transcription

Reference: Sahih al-Bukhari 7394, Sahih Muslim 2711

English

# 218 PRAYER FOR MERCY (BEFORE BEDTIME)

بِاسْمِكَ رَبِّي وَضَعْتُ جَنْبِي، وَبِكَ أَرْفَعُهُ، فَإِنْ أَمْسَكْتَ نَفْسِي فَارْحَمْهَا، وَإِنْ أَرْسَلْتَهَا فَاحْفَا، بِمَا تَحْفَظُ بِهِ عِبَادَكَ الصَّالِحِينَ.

Arabic

Bismika Rabbī waḍa`tu janbī, wa bika arfa`uh, fa in amsakta nafsī farḥamhā, wa in arsaltahā faḥfadhā bimā taḥfadu bihi `ibādaka ṣāliḥīn.

Phonetic transcription

With Your Name O Allah, I go to sleep and with Your Name I wake up. And if You take my soul, have mercy on it, and if You send it back then protect it as You protect Your righteous servants.

English

Reference: Al-Bukari 11.126

# 219 PRAYER FOR BLESSING THE DAY WAKING UP

اللَّهُمَّ بِكَ أَصْبَحْنَا، وَبِكَ أَمْسَيْنَا، وَبِكَ نَحْيَا، وَبِكَ نَمُوتُ، وَإِلَيْكَ النُّشُورُ.

Arabic

Allāhumma bika aṣbaḥnā, wa bika amsaynā, wa bika naḥyā, wa bika namūt, wa ilayka n-nushūr.

Phonetic transcription

O Allah, by You we enter the morning and by You we enter the evening, by You we live and by You we die, and to You is the Final Return.

English

Reference: Sahih At-Tirmidhi 3/142

# Prayers as part of religious acts

# 220 PRAYER FOR ANSWERING THE PRAYERS AFTER EVERY PRAYER

قُلْ هُوَ ٱللَّهُ أَحَدٌ، ٱللَّهُ ٱلصَّمَدُ، لَمْ يَلِدْ وَلَمْ يُولَدْ، وَلَمْ يَكُن لَّهُ كُفُوًا أَحَدُ.

Arabic

Qul huwa Llahu ahadun, Llahu ssamadu, Lam yalid walam yooladu, Walam yakun lahu kufuwan ahadu.

Say, He is Allah, who is One, Allah, the Eternal Refuge. He neither begets nor is born, Nor is there to Him any equivalent.

Phonetic transcription

Reference: Surat Al-Ikhlas (112)

English

# 221 PRAYER TO BLESS THE MESSENGER ﷺ

اللَّهُمَّ رَبَّ هَذِهِ الدَّعْوَةِ التَّامَّةِ، وَالصَّلاَةِ القَائِمَةِ آتِ مُحَمَّدًا الوَسِيلَةَ وَالفَضِيلَةَ، وَابْعَثْهُ مَقَامًا مَحْمُودًا الَّذِي وَعَدْتَهُ .

Arabic

Allāhumma rabba hādhihi 'd-da'wati 't-tāmmah wa ṣṣalāti 'l-qā'imah, 'āti Muhammadan 'l-wasīlata walfaḍīlata, wa b'ath-hu maqāma 'm-mahmūdan 'al-ladhī wa`adtahu.

O Allah , Lord of this perfect call and established prayer. Grant Muhammad the intercession and favor, and raise him to the honored station You have promised him.

Phonetic transcription

Reference: Al-Bukhari 1/152

English

# 222 PRAYER TO ALLAH WHEN RECITING THE QURAN

اللَّهمَّ اكتُب لي بِها عندَكَ أجرًا، وضَع عنِّي بِها وزرًا، واجعَلها لي عندَكَ ذُخرًا، وتقبَّلها منِّي كما تقبَّلتَها من عبدِكَ داودَ .

Arabic

Allāhumma k'tub lī bihā `indaka ajran, wamhu `annī bihā wizran, waj`alhā lī `indaka dhukhran, wa taqabbal'hā minnī kamā taqabbaltahā min `abdika Dāwūd.

O Allah, write it as a reward for me, and release me from a burden, and make it a treasure for me with You. Accept it from me as You accepted it from Your servant Dawud.

Phonetic transcription

Reference: At-Tirmidhi 2/473, and Al-Hakim who graded it authentic and Ath-Thahabi agreed 1/219

English

# 223 PRAYER FOR THE WELL-BEING OF THE PROPHET'S FAMILY

اللَّهُمَّ اجْعَلْ رِزْقَ آلِ مُحَمَّدٍ قُوتًا.

Arabic

Allahuma ijeal rizqa aali muhamadin qutan.

Phonetic transcription

Reference: Sunan Ibn Majah 4139

O Allah, make the provision of the family of Muhammad sufficient food.

English

# 224 PRAYER ON THE WAY TO THE MOSQUE

اللَّهُمَّ اجْعَلْ فِي قَلْبِي نُورًا، وَفِي بَصَرِي نُورًا، وَفِي سَمْعِي نُورًا، وَعَنْ يَمِينِي نُورًا، وَعَنْ يَسَارِي
نُورًا، وَفَوْقِي نُورًا، وَتَحْتِي نُورًا، وَأَمَامِي نُورًا، وَخَلْفِي نُورًااجْعَلْ لِي نُورًا.

Arabic

Allahumma ij'al fee qalbi nooran, wa fee basari nooran, wa fee sam'i nooran, wa 'an yameeni nooran, wa 'an yasari nooran, wa fawqi nooran, wa tahti nooran, wa amami nooran, wa khalfi nooran, wa ij'al li nooran.

Phonetic transcription

Reference: Al-Bukhari 11 / 116 (Hadith no. 6316) and by Muslim 1/526, 529-530 (Hadithno. 763)

O Allah, place light in my heart, light in my sight, light in my hearing, light on my right, light on my left, light above me, light beneath me, light in front of me, and light behind me. Grant me light.

English

# 225 PRAYER FOR ANSWERING THE PRAYERS (AT THE BEGINNING OF THE PRAYER)

إِنَّ صَلَاتِي وَنُسُكِي وَمَحْيَايَ وَمَمَاتِي لِلَّهِ رَبِّ الْعَالَمِينَ لَا شَرِيكَ لَهُ، وَبِذَلِكَ أُمِرْتُ وَأَنَا مِنَ الْمُسْلِمِينَ.
اللَّهُمَّ اهْدِنِي لِأَحْسَنِ الْأَعْمَالِ وَأَحْسَنِ الْأَخْلَاقِ لَا يَهْدِي لِأَحْسَنِهَا إِلَّا أَنْتَ، وَقِنِي سَيِّئَ الْأَعْمَالِ وَسَيِّئَ
الْأَخْلَاقِ لَا يَقِي سَيِّئَهَا إِلَّا أَنْتَ.

Arabic

'Inna salati wa nusuki wa mahyaya wa mamati lillahi rabbil-alamin, la sharika lahu, wa bi dhalika umirtu wa ana mina l-muslimin. Allahumma hdini li'ahsani l'amali wa ahsani l'akhlaqi la yahdi li ahsaniha illa anta wa qini sayy'a la'mali wa sayy'a l'akhlaqi la yaqi sayy'aha illa ant.

Phonetic transcription

Reference: Sunan an-Nasa'i 896

Indeed, my prayer, my rites of sacrifice, my living, and my dying are for Allah, Lord of the worlds. He has no partner. And of this I have been commanded, and I am one of the Muslims. O Allah, guide me to the best of deeds and the best of manners, for none guides to the best of them except You. Protect me from bad deeds and bad manners, for none can protect me from them except You.

English

## 226 PRAYER FOR STRONG FAITH (AT THE BEGINNING OF THE PRAYER)

اللَّهُمَّ لَكَ الْحَمْدُ أَنْتَ نُورُ السَّمَوَاتِ وَالْأَرْضِ وَلَكَ الْحَمْدُ أَنْتَ قَيَّامُ السَّمَوَاتِ وَالْأَرْضِ وَلَكَ الْحَمْدُ أَنْتَ
رَبُّ السَّمَوَاتِ وَالْأَرْضِ وَمَنْ فِيهِنَّ أَنْتَ الْحَقُّ وَوَعْدُكَ الْحَقُّ وَلِقَاؤُكَ حَقٌّ وَالْجَنَّةُ حَقٌّ وَالنَّارُ حَقٌّ
وَالسَّاعَةُ حَقٌّ اللَّهُمَّ لَكَ أَسْلَمْتُ وَبِكَ آمَنْتُ وَعَلَيْكَ تَوَكَّلْتُ وَإِلَيْكَ أَنَبْتُ وَبِكَ خَاصَمْتُ وَإِلَيْكَ حَاكَمْتُ
فَاغْفِرْ لِي مَا قَدَّمْتُ وَأَخَّرْتُ وَأَسْرَرْتُ وَأَعْلَنْتُ أَنْتَ إِلَهِي لَا إِلَّا أَنْتَ.

Arabic

Allahumma laka lhamdu anta nuru samawati wa l'ardi, wa laka lhamdu anta qayamu samawati wa l'ardi, wa laka lhamdu anta rabbu samawati wa l'ardi, waman fihina. Anta lhaqqu, wa qawluka lhaqqu, wa waduka lhaqqu, wa liqa'uka haqqun, wa ljannatu haqqun, wa nnaru haqqun, wa saatu haqqun. Allahumma laka aslamtu, wa bika amantu, wa alayka tawakaltu, wa ilayka anabtu, wa bika khasamtu, wa ilayka hakamtu, fa'ghfir li ma qadamtu wa akhartu wa asrartu, wa alantu. Anta llahiy, la ilaha illa ant.

Phonetic transcription

Reference: Sahih Muslim 769a

O Allah, praise belongs to You. You are the light of the heavens and the earth and praise belongs toYou.You are the Sustainer of the heavens and the earth and praise belongs to You. You are the Lord of the heavens and the earth and whoever is in them. You are the Truth, and Your words are true. Your promise is true, and the meeting with You is true. Paradise is true and Hell is true and the judgement day is true. O Allah, I submit toYou and I accept You and I trust in You and I turn to You and I argue by You and I summon toYou for judgement. Forgive me what I have done before me and what I would do after, what I have kept secret and what I have proclaimed, You are my god - there is no god but You.

English

## 227 PRAYER FOR REFUGE (WHEN ENTERING THE MOSQUE)

أَعُوذُ بِاللَّهِ الْعَظِيمِ وَبِوَجْهِهِ الْكَرِيمِ وَسُلْطَانِهِ الْقَدِيمِ مِنَ الشَّيْطَانِ الرَّجِيمِ.

Arabic

'A`ūdhu billihi l-`adīm, wa bi wajhihi l-karīm, wa sultānihi l-qadīm, mina shaytāni rrajīm.

Phonetic transcription

Reference: Abu Dawud 1/126

I seek refuge in Allah, the Mighty, and in His noble countenance, and in His eternal authority, from the accursed Satan.

English

## 228 PRAYER FOR PROTECTION FROM THE DEVIL (AT THE BEGINNING OF THE PRAYER)

اللَّهُمَّ إِنِّي أَعُوذُ بِكَ مِنَ الشَّيْطَانِ الرَّجِيمِ، وَهَمْزِهِ، وَنَفْخِهِ، وَنَفْثِهِ.

Arabic

Allahumma inni a'udhu bika minash-Shaitanir-rajim, wa hamzihi wa nafkhihi wa nafthihi.

Phonetic transcription

Reference: Sunan Ibn Majah 808

I seek refuge with You, O Allah, from the accursed Satan, his cunning, his blowing, and his spitting.

English

## 229 PRAYER FOR FORGIVENESS OF SINS (BY PROSTRATION)

اللهُمَّ اغْفِرْ لِي ذَنْبِي كُلَّهُ دِقَّهُ، وَجِلَّهُ، وَأَوَّلَهُ وَآخِرَهُ وَعَلَانِيَتَهُ وَسِرَّهُ.

Arabic

Allāhumma ghfir lī dhanbī kullahu, diqqahu wa jillahu, wa awalahu wa ākhirahu wa `alāniyatahu wa sirrahu.

O Allah, forgive me all my sins, great and small, the first and the last, those that are apparent and those that are hidden.

Reference: Muslim 1/350

Phonetic transcription

English

## 230 PRAYER FOR REFUGE (BY PROSTRATION)

اللهُمَّ أَعُوذُ بِرِضَاكَ مِنْ سَخَطِكَ، وَبِمُعَافَاتِكَ مِنْ عُقُوبَتِكَ، وَأَعُوذُ بِكَ مِنْكَ لَا أُحْصِي ثَنَاءً عَلَيْكَ أَنْتَكَمَا أَثْنَيْتَ عَلَى نَفْسِكَ.

Arabic

Allāhumma innī a`ūdhu biriḍāka min sakhaṭik, wa bimu`āfātika min `uqūbatik wa a`ūdhu bika minka lā uḥṣī thanā'an `alayka anta kamā athnayta `alā nafsika.

O Allah, I seek refuge in Your pleasure from Your displeasure, and I seek refuge in Your pardon from Your punishment. I seek refuge in You from You. I cannot praise You enough; You are as You have praised Yourself.

Reference: Muslim 1/352

Phonetic transcription

English

## 231 PRAYER FOR PROTECTION FROM DISBELIEF (AFTER PRAYER)

اللَّهُمَّ إِنِّي أَعُوذُ بِكَ مِنَ الْكُفْرِ وَالْفَقْرِ وَعَذَابِ الْقَبْرِ.

Arabic

Allāhumma innī a`ūdhu bika mina l-kufri, wa l-faqri, wa a`ūdhu bika min `adhābi l-qabr.

O Allah, I seek refuge in You from disbelief and poverty, and I seek refuge in You from the punishment of the grave.

Reference: Abu Dawud 4/324, Ahmad 5/42

Phonetic transcription

English

## 232 PRAYER FOR FORGIVENESS OF SINS (AFTER TASHAHHUD)

اللَّهُمَّ إِنِّي ظَلَمْتُ نَفْسِي ظُلْمًا كَثِيرًا وَلَا يَغْفِرُ الذُّنُوبَ إِلَّا أَنْتَ فَاغْفِرْ لِي مَغْفِرَةً مِنْ عِنْدِكَ وَارْحَمْنِي إِنَّكَ أَنْتَ الْغَفُورُ الرَّحِيمُ.

Arabic

Allāhumma 'innī dalamtu nafsī dulman kathīran, wa lā yaghfiru dhunūba illā 'anta, faghfir lī maghfiratam'min `indika warḥamnī innaka 'anta l-Ghafūr ur-Rahīm.

Phonetic transcription

O Allah, I have wronged myself greatly, and none forgives sins except You. So forgive me with a forgiveness from You and have mercy upon me. Surely, You are the Most Forgiving, Most Merciful.

English

Reference: Al-Bukhari 8/168, Muslim 4/2078

## 233 PRAYER FOR ENTERING PARADISE (AFTER TASHAHHUD)

اللَّهُمَّ إِنِّي أَسْأَلُكَ الْجَنَّةَ وَأَعُوذُ بِكَ مِنَ النَّارِ.

Arabic

Allāhumma innī as'aluka 'l-jannah wa a`ūdhu bika mina n-nār.

Phonetic transcription

O Allah, I ask You for Paradise, and I seek Your protection from Hell.

English

Reference: Abu Dawud. See also Al-Albani, Sahih Ibn Majah 2/328

## 234 PRAYER FOR FORGIVENESS (AFTER PRAYER)

اللَّهُمَّ إِنِّي أَسْأَلُكَ يَا أَللَّهُ بِأَنَّكَ الْوَاحِدُ الْأَحَدُ الصَّمَدُ الَّذِي لَمْ يَلِدْ وَلَمْ يُولَدْ وَلَمْ يَكُنْ لَهُ كُفُوًا أَحَدٌ أَنْ تَغْفِرَ لِي ذُنُوبِي إِنَّكَ أَنْتَ الْغَفُورُ الرَّحِيمُ.

Arabic

Allāhumma innī as'aluka yā Allāh bi 'annaka l-Wāḥidu laḥadu ṣamadu, alladhī lam yalid wa lam yūlad, wa lam yakun lahu kufuwan aḥad, an taghfira lī dhunūbī, innaka anta 'l-Ghafūrur-Raḥīm.

Phonetic transcription

O Allah, I ask You, O Allah, for You are the One, the Unique, the Self-Sufficient Master, who begets not, nor was begotten, and there is none comparable to Him. Forgive my sins, for You are the Most Forgiving, Most Merciful.

English

Reference: An-Nasa'i 3/52, Ahmad 4/338. See also Al-Albani, Sahih An-Nasa'i 1/280 and Sifat Salatun-Nabi, pg. 204

## 235 PRAYER FOR THE RIGHT PATH (FOR NIGHT PRAYER)

اللَّهُمَّ اغْفِرْ لِي وَاهْدِنِي وَارْزُقْنِي وَعَافِنِي.

Arabic

Allāhumma'ghfir lī, wahdinī, warzuqnī, wa `āfinī.

O Allah, forgive me, guide me, grant me sustenance, and bless me with well-being.

Phonetic transcription

Reference: Abu Dawud, Ibn Majah, At-Tirmidhi. See also Al-Albani, Sahih At-Tirmidhi 1/90 and Sahih Ibn Majah 1/148

English

## 236 PRAYER FOR PROTECTION FROM EVIL (AFTER PRAYER)

قُلْ أَعُوذُ بِرَبِّ ٱلْفَلَقِ، مِن شَرِّ مَا خَلَقَ، وَمِن شَرِّ غَاسِقٍ إِذَا وَقَبَ، وَمِن شَرِّ ٱلنَّفَّٰثَٰتِ فِي ٱلْعُقَدِ، وَمِن شَرِّ حَاسِدٍ إِذَا حَسَدَ.

Arabic

Qul a'udhu bi Rabbi l-Falaq, min sharri ma khalaq, wa min sharri ghasiqin idha waqab, wa min sharri an-naffathati fi al'uqad, wa min sharri hasidin idha hasad.

Say: I seek refuge in the Lord of the daybreak, from the evil of that which He created, from the evil of the darkness when it is intense, and from the evil of malignant witchcraft, and from the evil of an envier when he envies.

Phonetic transcription

Reference: Surat Al-Falaq (113)

English

## 237 PRAYER FOR PROTECTION (UPON LEAVING THE MOSQUE)

اللَّهُمَّ اعْصِمْنِي مِنَ الشَّيْطَانِ الرَّجِيمِ.

Arabic

Allāhumma`ṣimni mina shaytāni rajīm.

O Allah, protect me from Satan the outcast.

Phonetic transcription

Reference: Sunan Ibn Majah 773

English

# 238 PRAYER FOR FOR ALLAH'S MERCY (UPON ENTERING THE MOSQUE)

اللَّهُمَّ افْتَحْ لِي أَبْوَابَ رَحْمَتِكَ.

Arabic

Allāhumma ftaḥ lī 'abwāba raḥmatik.

O Allah, open for me the doors of Your mercy.

Phonetic transcription

Reference: Sahih Ibn Majah 1/128-9

English

# 239 PRAYER FOR PURIFICATION (UPON COMPLETING THE ABLUTION)

اللَّهُمَّ اجْعَلْنِي مِنَ التَّوَّابِينَ وَاجْعَلْنِي مِنَ المتَطَهِّرِينَ.

Arabic

Allāhumma j`alnī mina ttawwābīna wa j`alnī mina l-mutaṭahhirīn.

O Allah, make me among those who turn to You in repentance, and make me among those who are purified.

Phonetic transcription

Reference: At-Tirmidhi 1/78. See also Al-Albani, Sahih At- Tirmidhi 1/18

English

# 240 PRAYER AT THE START OF THE PRAYER (AFTER TAKBEER)

اللَّهُمَّ رَبَّ جَبْرَائِيلَ وَمِيكَائِيلَ وَإِسْرَافِيلَ فَاطِرَ السَّمَاوَاتِ وَالْأَرْضِ عَالِمَ الْغَيْبِ وَالشَّهَادَةِ أَنْتَ تَحْكُمُ بَيْنَ عِبَادِكَ فِيمَا كَانُوا فِيهِ يَخْتَلِفُونَ اهْدِنِي لِمَا اخْتُلِفَ فِيهِ مِنَ الْحَقِّ بِإِذْنِكَ إِنَّكَ تَهْدِي مَنْ تَشَاءُ إِلَى صِرَاطٍ مُسْتَقِيمٍ.

Arabic

Allāhumma rabba jabrā'īla, wa mīkā'īla, wa isrāfīla fāṭira samāwāti wa 'l-arḍi, ` ālima lghaybi wa shahādati, anta taḥkumu bayna `ibādika fīmā kānū fīhi yakhtalifūna. Ihdinī lima khtulifa fīhi min alḥaqqi bi idhnika. Innaka tahdī man tashā'u ilā ṣirāṭin mustaqīm.

O Allah, Lord of Jibraīl, Mīkaīl and Israfīl, Creator of the heavens and the Earth, Knower of the seen and the unseen. You are the arbitrator between Your servants in that which they have disputed. Guide me to the truth by Your leave, in that which they have differed, for verily You guide whom You will to a straight path.

Phonetic transcription

Reference: Muslim 1/534

English

## 241 PRAYER FOR BLESSINGS AND PROTECTION (WITR PRAYER)

اللَّهُمَّ اهْدِنِي فِيمَنْ هَدَيْتَ وَعَافِنِي فِيمَنْ عَافَيْتَ وَتَوَلَّنِي فِيمَنْ تَوَلَّيْتَ وَبَارِكْ لِي أَعْطَيْتَ وَقِنِي شَرَّ مَا قَضَيْتَ إِنَّكَ تَقْضِي وَلاَ يُقْضَى عَلَيْكَ وَإِنَّهُ لاَ يَذِلُّ مَنْ وَالَيْتَ وَلاَ يَعِزُّ مَنْ عَادَيْتَ تَبَارَكْتَ رَبَّنَا وَتَعَالَيْتَ.

Arabic

Allahumma hdini fiman hadayta wa 'afini fiman afayt wa tawallani fiman tawallayt wa barik li fima a'tayt, wa qini sharra ma qadayt, innaka taqdi wa la yuqda 'alayk, wa innahu la yadhillu man walayt, tabarakta Rabbana wa at'alayt.

Reference: Sunan an-Nasa'i 1745

O Allah, guide me among those You have guided, pardon me among those You have pardoned, turn me into good health among those You have turned into good health, befriend me among those You have befriended, and bless me in what You have given. Protect me from the evil You have decreed, for You decree and none could influence You. Indeed, he whom You show allegiance to is never abased, and he whom You take as an enemy is never honored. Blessed are You, our Lord, and Exalted.

Phonetic transcription

English

## 242 PRAYER FOR SUPPORT AND FORGIVENESS (WITR PRAYER)

اللهُمَّ إِنَّا نَسْتَعِينُكَ وَنَسْتَغْفِرُكَ، وَنُؤْمِنُ بِكَ، وَنَخْضَعُ لَكَ، وَنَخْلَعُ وَنَتْرُكُ مَنْ يَكْفُرُكَ، اللهُمَّ إِيَّاكَ نَعْبُدُ، وَلَكَ نُصَلِّي وَنَسْجُدُ وَإِلَيْكَ نَسْعَى وَنَحْفِدُ، وَنَرْجُو رَحْمَتَكَ وَنَخْشَى عَذَابَكَ، وَنَخَافُ عَذَابَكَ الْجِدَّ إِنَّ عَذَابَكَ بِالْكَافِرِينَ مُلْحِقٌ.

Arabic

Allāhumma iyāka na`bud, wa laka nuṣallī wa nasjud, wa ilayka nas`ā wa naḥfid, narjū raḥmatak, wa nakhshā `adhābak, inna `adhābaka bilkāfirīna mulḥaq. Allāhumma innā nasta`īnuk, wa nastaghfiruk, wa nuthnī `alayka lkhayr, wa lā nakfuruk, wa nu'minu bik, wa nakhḍa`u lak, wa nakhla`u man yakfuruk.

Reference: Al-Bayhaqi graded its chain authentic in As-Sunan Al-Kubra. Al-Albani said in 'Irwa'ul-Ghalil 2/170 that its chain is authentic as a statement of 'Umar.

O Allah, You alone we worship, and to You, we pray and prostrate. To You, we strive and for You, we seek refuge and fear. We hope for Your mercy and fear Your punishment, for surely, Your punishment is due upon the disbelievers. O Allah, we seek Your help and ask for Your forgiveness. We praise You for your goodness. We believe and submit to You. We surrender to You and reject those who disbelieve in You.

Phonetic transcription

English

## 243 PRAYER WHEN BREAKING FAST IN SOMEONE'S HOME

أَفْطَرَ عِنْدَكُمُ الصَّائِمُونَ، وأَكَلَ طَعَامَكُمُ الأَبْرَارُ، وَصَلَّتْ عَلَيْكُمُ الْمَلَائِكَةُ.

Arabic

Afṭara `indakumu ṣā'imūn, wa akala ṭa`āmakumu l'abrār, wa ṣallat `alaykumu lmalā'ika.

Reference: Abu Dawud 3/367, Ibn Majah 1/556, An-Nasa'i, 'Amalul-Yawm wal-Laylah 296-8. Al-Albani graded it authentic in Sahih Abu Dawud 2/730

The fasting have broken their fast in your presence, the righteous have eaten your food, and the angels have invoked blessings upon you.

Phonetic transcription

English

## 244 PRAYER TO PROTECT YOURSELF FROM BREAKING THE FAST

إِذَا دُعِيَ أَحَدُكُمْ فَلْيُجِبْ، فإنْ كانَ صَائِمًا فَلْيُصَلِّ، وإنْ كانَ مُفْطِرًا فَلْيَطْعَمْ.

Arabic

Idha du'iya ahadikum falyujib, fa'in kana sa'iman falyusalli, wa-in kana mufatiran falya'tam.

When one of you is invited, respond to the invitation. If you are fasting, then perform the prayer; and if you are not fasting, then eat.

Reference: Muslim 2/1054

Phonetic transcription

English

## 245 PRAYER FOR RIGHTEOUSNESS ON THE DAY OF ARAFAH

خَيْرُ الدعاءُ يَوْمِ عَرَفَةَ، وَخَيْرُ مَا قُلْتُ أَنَا وَالنبيونَ مِنْ قَبْلِي: لا إِلَهَ إِلَّا اللهُ وَحْدَهُ لَرِيكَ لَهُ، لَهُ الْمُلْكُ وَلَهُ الْحَمْدُ وَهُوَ عَلَى كُلِّ شَيْءٍ قَدِيرٌ .

Arabic

Lā ilāha illallāh, waḥdahu lā sharīka lahu, lahul-mulku wa lahul-ḥamdu, wa huwa 'alā kulli shai'in qadīr.

None has the right to be worshiped but Allah, alone without partner. To Him belongs all that exists, and to Him is the praise, and He is powerful over all things.

Reference: Jami' at-Tirmidhi 3585

Phonetic transcription

English

## 246 PRAYER UPON BEING AT SAFA AND MARWA

لاَ إِلَهَ إِلَّا اللهُ وَحْدَهُ لا شَرِيكَ لَهُ، لَهُ الْمُلْكُ وَلَهُ الْحَمْدُ وَهُوَ عَلَى كُلِّ شَيْءٍ قَدِيرٌ، لاَ إِلَهَ إلا اللَّهُ وَحْدَهُ أَنْجَزَ وَعْدَهُ، وَنَصرَ عَبْدَهُ وَهَزَمَ الأَحْزَابَ وَحْدَهُ.

Arabic

Lā ilāha 'illallāh waḥdahu lā sharīka lah, lahu 'l-mulku wa lahu 'l-ḥamd wa huwa `alā kulli shay'in qadīr, lā 'ilāha illallāhu waḥdahu, anjaza wa`dah, wa naṣara `abdah, wa hazama 'l 'aḥzāba waḥdah.

There is no god but Allah, alone without any partner. To Him belongs all things, and to Him is all praise, and He is able to do all things. There is no god but Allah alone. He fulfilled His promise, granted victory to His servant, and He alone defeated the confederates.

Reference: Muslim 2/888

Phonetic transcription

English

## 247 PRAYER BETWEEN THE YAMAANI CORNER AND THE BLACK STONE IN THE KA'BAH'

رَبَّنَآ ءَاتِنَا فِي ٱلدُّنْيَا حَسَنَةً وَفِي ٱلْأَخِرَةِ حَسَنَةً وَقِنَا عَذَابَ ٱلنَّارِ.

Arabic

Rabbana atina fi ddunya hasanah wa fi lakhirati hasanah wa qina 'adhaba an-nar.

O Allah, give us the good of this world and the good of the Hereafter, and save us from the punishment of Hell.

Phonetic transcription

Reference: Surat Al-Baqarah (2:201)

English

## 248 PRAYER UPON BREAKING FAST (IFTAR)

ذَهَبَ الظَّمَأُ وَابْتَلَّتِ الْعُرُوقُ وَثَبَتَ الْأَجْرُ إِنْ شَاءَ اللهُ.

Arabic

Dhahaba dama', wabtallati l-`urūq, wa thabata l-'ajru in shā' Allāh.

The thirst is gone, the veins are moistened, and the reward is confirmed, if Allah wills.

Phonetic transcription

Reference: Abu Dawud 2/306 and others. See also Al- Albani, Sahihul-Jami' As-Saghir 4/209

English

## 249 PRAYER AT NIGHT OF DECREE (LAILAT-UL-QADR)

اللَّهُمَّ إِنَّكَ عَفُوٌّ تُحِبُّ الْعَفْوَ فَاعْفُ عَنِّي.

Arabic

Allahumma innaka 'afuwun tuhibbu l-'afwa, fa'fu 'anni.

O Allah, You are Forgiving and love forgiveness, so forgive me.

Phonetic transcription

Reference: Sunan Ibn Majah 3850

English

## 250 PRAYER IN THE MONTH OF RAJAB

اللَّهمَّ بارِكْ لَنا في رجبٍ وشعبانَ وبلِّغنا رمضانَ.

Arabic

Allahuma barik lana fi rajab washaeban wa balighna ramadan.

O Allah, bless us in Rajab and Sha'ban, and allow us to reach Ramadan.

Reference: Mishkat al-Masabih 1369

Phonetic transcription

English

# Praises

# 251 PRAISING ALLAH FOR HIS ALMIGHTY MAJESTY

ٱللَّهُ لَآ إِلَٰهَ إِلَّا هُوَ ٱلۡحَيُّ ٱلۡقَيُّومُۚ لَا تَأۡخُذُهُۥ سِنَةٞ وَلَا نَوۡمٞۚ لَّهُۥ مَا فِي ٱلسَّمَٰوَٰتِ وَمَا فِي ٱلۡأَرۡضِۗ مَن ذَا ٱلَّذِي يَشۡفَعُ عِندَهُۥٓ إِلَّا بِإِذۡنِهِۦۚ يَعۡلَمُ مَا بَيۡنَ أَيۡدِيهِمۡ وَمَا خَلۡفَهُمۡۖ وَلَا يُحِيطُونَ بِشَيۡءٖ مِّنۡ عِلۡمِهِۦٓ إِلَّا بِمَا شَآءَۚ وَسِعَ كُرۡسِيُّهُ ٱلسَّمَٰوَٰتِ وَٱلۡأَرۡضَۖ وَلَا يَـُٔودُهُۥ حِفۡظُهُمَاۚ وَهُوَ ٱلۡعَلِيُّ ٱلۡعَظِيمُ .

Arabic

Allahu la ilaha illa huwa alhayu alqayyoom la takhuthuhu sinatun wala nawm lahu ma fee samawati wama fee lardi man dha llathee yashfa'u 'indahu illa bi'idhnihi ya'lamu ma bayna aydihim wama khalfahum wala yuhitoona bishay'in min 'ilmihi illa bima shaa wasi'a kursiyuhu samawati wa l'arda wala yaoduhu hifdhuhuma wahuwa al'aliyyu al'adhim.

Phonetic transcription

Reference: Surat Al-Baqarah (2:255)

Allah, there is no deity except Him, the Ever-Living, the Sustainer of all existence. Neither drowsiness overtakes Him nor sleep. To Him belongs whatever is in the heavens and whatever is on the earth. Who is it that can intercede with Him except by His permission? He knows what is before them and what will be after them, and they encompass not a thing of His knowledge except for what He wills. His Kursi extends over the heavens and the earth, and their preservation tires Him not. And He is the Most High, the Most Great.

English

# 252 PRAISING ALLAH FOR HIS RIGHTEOUSNESS

الْحَمْدُ لِلَّهِ الَّذِي بِنِعْمَتِهِ تَتِمُّ الصَّالِحَاتُ.

Arabic

Alḥamdu lillāhi ladi bi ni`matihi tatimmu ṣāliḥāt.

Phonetic transcription

Reference: Al-Albani, Sahihul-Jami' As-Saghir 4/201

Praise is to Allah Who by His blessings all good things are perfected.

English

# 253 PRAISING ALLAH IN THE EVENING

سُبْحَانَ اللَّهِ رَبِّ الْعَالَمِينَ، سُبْحَانَ اللَّهِ وَبِحَمْدِهِ.

Arabic

Subhan Allahi Rabbi l 'alami, Subhan Allahi wa bihamdihi.

Phonetic transcription

Reference: Sunan Ibn Majah 3879

Glory is to Allah, the Lord of the worlds, glory and praise is to Allah.

English

## 254 PRAISING ALLAH AFTER EVERY PRAYER

سُبْحَانَ اللهِ وَالْحَمْدُ لِلَّهِ وَلَا إِلَهَ إِلَّا اللَّهُ وَاللَّهُ أَكْبَرُ.

Arabic

Subḥān Allāh, walḥamdu li Llāh, wa lā ilāha illa Llāh, wa Llāhu 'Akbar.

Phonetic transcription

Reference: Sahih Muslim 2137

Glory is to Allah, and praise is to Allah, and there is none worthy of worship but Allah, and Allah is the Most Great.

English

## 255 PRAISING ALLAH IN THE MORNING

اللَّهُمَّ بِكَ أَصْبَحْنَا، وَبِكَ أَمْسَيْنَا، وَبِكَ نَحْيَا، وَبِكَ نَمُوتُ، وَإِلَيْكَ النُّشُورُ.

Arabic

Allāhumma bika aṣbaḥnā, wa bika amsaynā, wa bika naḥyā, wa bika namūt, wa ilayka nnushūr.

Phonetic transcription

Reference: Sahih At-Tirmidhi 3/142

O Allah, by You we enter the morning and by You we enter the evening, by You we live and by You we die, and to You is the Final Return.

English

## 256 PRAISING ALLAH FOR HIS GOODNESS

الحمدُ للهِ حمدًا كثيرًا طيِّبًا مُبارَكًا فيه غيرَ مَكفيٍّ ولا مودَّعٍ ولا مستغنًى عنه رَبَّنَا.

Arabic

Alhamdu lillāhi ḥamdan kathīran tayyiban mubārakan fīh, ghayra makfiyin wa lā muwadda`in, wa lā mustaghnan `anhu Rabbanā.

Phonetic transcription

Reference: Al-Bukhari 6/214, At-Tirmidhi 5/507

Praise be to Allah, abundant, pure, and blessed praise that is neither insufficient nor transient. Our Lord, we are not capable of praising You enough, nor can we ever be independent of You.

English

## 257 PRAISE ALLAH IN JOY

اللهُ أَكْبَرُ.

Arabic

Allāhu Akbar.

Allah is the Greatest.

Phonetic transcription

Reference: Al-Bukhari, cf. Al-Asqalani, Fathul-Bari 8/441. See also Al-Albani, Sahih At-Tirmidhi 2/103, 235, Ahmad 5/218

English

## 258 PRAISING ALLAH UPON ASTONISHMENT & SURPRISE

سُبْحَانَ اللهِ.

Arabic

Subḥāna Llāh.

Glory is to Allah.

Phonetic transcription

Reference: Al-Bukhari, cf. Al-Asqalani, Fathul-Bari 1/210, 390, 414 and Muslim 4/1857

English

## 259 PRAISING ALLAH AFTER EATING

الْحَمْدُ لِلَّهِ الَّذِي أَطْعَمَنِي هَذَا الطَّعَامَ وَرَزَقَنِيهِ مِنْ غَيْرِ حَوْلٍ مِنِّي وَلاَ قُوَّةٍ.

Arabic

Alhamdu li Llāhi ladhī aṭ`amanī hādhā ṭa`ama, wa razaqanīhi min ghayri ḥawlin minnī wa lā quwah.

Praise be to Allah who has given me this food without any effort or power from my part.

Phonetic transcription

Reference: At-Tirmidhi, Abu Dawud, and Ibn Majah. See also Al-Albani, Sahih At-Tirmidhi 3/159

English

# Profession of faith

## 260 THE PROFESSION OF FAITH IN ISLAM (THE SHAHADA)

أَشْهَدُ أَنْ لاَ إِلَهَ إِلاَّ اللَّهُ وأَشْهَدُ أَنَّ مُحَمَّدًا عَبْدُهُ وَرَسُولُهُ.

Arabic

Ash-hadu an la ilaha illallah, wa ash-hadu anna Muhammadan rasulullah.

Phonetic transcription

I testify There is no deity but Allah and I testify Muhammad is the Messenger of Allah.

English

Reference: Sunan an-Nasa'i 632 and Sunan Ibn Majah 470

# Epilogue

We have come to the end of this book, but our worship of the Almighty does not end here. If we want to be close to Allah, we must invoke and praise Him regularly as part of the prayers. In addition, we use dua in certain situations to pay homage to Allah, thank Him and live in accordance with the scriptures and Islamic laws. We have also used creeds and praises to thank the Almighty and prove to Him our established faith.

It is now our duty to spread the wisdom of Allah. In this way, family members, relatives and friends can also seek closeness to the Almighty and lead a more fulfilling life in the spirit of Islam. In the spirit of Allah, we should give this book to those we love.

May God be with you.

ليكن الله معك

ISLAM
WAY

Dear reader,

Did you like the book?

Perhaps you need help with playing audio files?

We welcome your honest comments, are always open to criticism and are happy to help.

Please do not hesitate to send us an email at info@islamway-books.com.

Yours sincerely

Ibrahim Al-Abadi & Islam Way

Printed in Great Britain
by Amazon

41010505R00066